THEMES
NEW PLAYS FOR NATIONA

TABOOS

JOHN MURRAY

ABOUT THIS BOOK

There are five playscripts in this book. All five are about *Taboos*. They are about subjects that people often find difficult to discuss . . . things like love, illness, adoption, growing old and death.

There may be people in your class who also find it difficult to talk about these things. It's important to respect their feelings. Don't force them to join in if they don't want to!

The plays have a lot of characters, so there's a good chance that everyone in the class will get to take a part.

You can read them aloud in lesson time, or rehearse them for performing to others. You'll find hints on the best ways of reading and performing in 'Using the Scripts'. If this is the first time you've used this book, we suggest that you read through the whole section.

At the end of each script, you'll also find some **Talking points** – discussing the ideas in the play; and a list of **Investigations** with ideas for project work in English, drama, technology . . . and more.

© Series arrangement and editorial text: Alan Lambert & June Mitchell

The Sympathy Card © Kevin Fegan

The Birthday Present © Janys Chambers

Bullseye © Maria Oshodi

The Last Cuckoo © John Wood

All Souls' Eve © Nona Shepphard

First published 1990
by John Murray (Publishers) Ltd
50 Albemarle St, London W1X 4BD

Cover illustration by David Anstey
Typeset by Phoenix Photosetting, Chatham, Kent
Printed and bound in Great Britain by Biddles of Guildford

British Library Cataloguing in Publication Data

Taboos. – (Themescripts series)
  1. Drama in English, 1945 –
  Anthologies
I. Series
822. 91408

ISBN 0–7195–4805–5

CONTENTS

Using the Scripts   4

The Sympathy Card   Kevin Fegan   9
  Talking Points and Investigations   29

The Birthday Present   Janys Chambers   33
  Talking Points and Investigations   53

Bullseye   Maria Oshodi   57
  Talking Points and Investigations   76

The Last Cuckoo   John Wood   80
  Talking Points and Investigations   100

All Souls' Eve   Nona Shepphard   104
  Talking Points and Investigations   130

USING THE SCRIPTS

The playscripts have been written mainly for reading in class. Each of you can take a part or maybe share a part. They can also be learned, rehearsed and performed in front of an audience so each script has stage directions to help you present the plays.

Each play can be read straight through in about 30–40 minutes.

You'll find a cast list at the beginning of each script which lists the characters in the play. The characters with most to say – or those with very complicated speeches – appear first on the cast list. The cast list will also tell you whether characters are male or female. You'll find that most characters could be played by a girl or a boy without making any difference to the sense of the play.

Someone will need to read out the stage directions (the lines in italics). These let everyone know where and when a particular scene is supposed to be taking place. They also provide a kind of linking commentary which holds the story together.

Whether you read the plays in lesson time or prepare them for performance, remember that the most important thing is to bring the script to life. It's your job to 'lift' the characters off the page and to make them talk and behave as real people.

Here are some hints that may help you in your task.

Reading Aloud

Playscripts can sometimes look very confusing! The lines are very often of different lengths and seem to be broken up more than they are in a novel or a textbook.

The characters' names are listed down the side of the page. When you're reading a character you have to read ahead a little to see when your next speech is coming up. If you don't, you'll find that there are long pauses – and maybe groans – while the rest of the class waits for you to realise that it's your turn to read. You will sometimes have time to prepare your next speech while the stage directions are being read out.

Even professional actors sometimes have difficulty in reading a script out loud when they haven't had a chance to read it first. Why should it be any easier for you? Well . . . it won't be, but there are some tricks you can use to help the reading go more smoothly, and to help the play spring into life.

Skip-reading

If there's time at the beginning of the lesson, start reading through the play to yourself. Even if you only manage to 'skip' through the first couple of scenes, it will give you an idea of the characters, the way they speak, the kind of language the writer is using, and the general layout of the script. You'll also begin to get some idea of the play's style. Is it funny, serious, realistic, fantastical? Is the situation one that's new to you? What are the characters like? Do you know people like them? You can discuss these points before you all get down to reading the play together. Ten minutes skip-reading will lead to a more lively and enjoyable session.

You can skip-read with a partner, each of you taking alternate lines. If there was time you could probably work your way through the entire play like this.

Searching out the tricky bits

You'll need preparation time for this too! Instead of skip-reading the opening scenes, flick through the entire play. Watch out for any difficult or unfamiliar words. If you've already been given a character to read, just go through your own lines. Otherwise, help out with a general search and don't forget to watch out for tricky stage directions.

Occasionally the play will ask your character to sing a song. Sing it if you know the tune, but otherwise read it out as if it were a poem.

Quick character sketches

If you've never seen these plays before, how can you find out about the character you've been asked to read? You'll find some help in the cast list at the start of each script. As you read you'll obviously get to know more about him or her; the speeches will give you clues as to what the character is like. You can also get help from your teacher. The chances are that they will know the script well and may have used it with other groups before.

Ask about your character. Maybe even ask for a demonstration of how your teacher sees the character. How would they begin to play it?

Reading ahead

Learn the trick of reading ahead . . . of letting your eyes move on a couple of lines when another character is speaking, so that you're ready with your speech when your turn comes.

This is not always easy because you've still got to concentrate on what other people are saying. If you don't, you're likely to lose your place completely. With practice, though, you may find yourself becoming a very smooth play reader.

You'll also need to use the same kind of skill/technique when you're reading a speech that carries over from one line to the next. Don't pause at the end of the line *unless* it is also the end of a sentence, otherwise it will make for a real stop–start performance.

Watching for signals

As you read ahead you'll also need to watch for the signals the writer gives you on how to read your lines.

So when you see commas and full stops don't be afraid to pause. Dashes '–' or a series of dots '. . .' also mean you should pause. Don't be shy about giving real feeling to a sentence that ends with an exclamation mark! Where a writer tells you that a character whispers . . . whisper. Where you read that a character shouts . . . SHOUT!

Enjoy making your speeches lively or dramatic or funny or frightened . . . or whatever it is they're supposed to be. Put as much expression as you can into the reading, because if *you* do, the chances are that you'll encourage your classmates to do the same. Plays are meant for sharing.

Looking forwards and backwards

It can be very useful to stop the reading for a few seconds at a suitable moment and discuss together as a class what you think is going to happen next. In the same way, after some complicated action you can pause to discuss what has happened so far.

Second readings

Once you're through the first reading, and if you've enjoyed what the play is saying – or even if there are ideas there that you don't yet understand – there's the possibility of a second reading.

You may not want to go through the whole play but perhaps there are one or two sections that you'd like to read again or deal with in greater detail. A second reading also gives you the chance to swap the parts around.

Performing the Plays

Some people enjoy performing a play to an audience; on the other hand, some people hate the idea!

If you've only got a limited amount of time to get a performance ready, it will be better to choose just one or two scenes and really concentrate on doing these well.

For some performances you'll need to write to the publishers for permission. Details are at the beginning of the book.

If you decide to prepare one of these scripts for performance, then you'll need to give some thought to the kind of performance it's going to be.

Here are some of your choices.

Performing 'live': making a piece of theatre

If you're going to make a 'live' performance where are you going to present it? On a stage? In the round — with the audience sitting on all sides of the acting area? In a corner of a classroom?

Are you going to have elaborate settings and costumes, or will you keep the whole event very simple? Most of the plays in this book allow for very simple staging.

Are you going to have stage lighting? If so, would this be the most effective way of changing scenes?

You could do a rehearsed reading. You don't need to learn the lines and work out moves for this because you sit and read the play to your audience. But go through the play several times together first, so that you can give the reading real expression!

Making a video

If you have the use of a video camera, can you adapt the script for showing as a television play? If so, will you simply point the camera at the scene, or will you want to experiment with close-ups and long shots and camera angles? Will you need to rewrite the script as a 'shooting script'?

As with a live performance, you'll have to think about the kind of settings and costumes you're going to use. Will you need to film 'on location' to give your presentation the kind of realistic feel that looks good on television? Some of the plays in this collection lend themselves well to location work; there are scenes set in classrooms, playgrounds, houses, streets, playing fields and churchyards.

Making a radio play

Recording a play on tape looks the simplest choice of all. Certainly you won't have to worry about costumes, settings, lighting or complicated moves. But there are some details that you ought to bear in mind as you prepare for this type of presentation.

How many microphones are you going to use? Where are you going to position them to get the best effect? Remember that your actors need to be able to get to a microphone easily when it's their turn to speak.

Have you got a recording room where you can keep out unwanted sounds? Will you want to record 'on location'? Some of the plays would make for very realistic-sounding radio productions if you were able to record them in and around your school and neighbourhood.

Do any of your actors' voices sound the same? If so you may be heading for trouble, because your listeners won't be able to tell which character is speaking. Choose a range of voices to make for variety and to avoid confusion.

So . . . what kind of presentation will you choose to make? One advantage of the video and radio versions is that they can often be less nerve-racking for those people who don't like getting up and performing in front of an audience. And for those people who can't even stand the sight of themselves on video, the radio play has got to be the best choice of all!

Whichever you choose, the actor's job is to make the piece come to life. The words on the paper need to be given flesh and blood – *yours!* In the time that you've got available, do as much work as you can on your character. How do they look and sound? What's their history? What kind of place do they live in? Do you know anyone who looks or acts like them?

If you don't want to act you could be a director, stage manager, camera operator, musician, sound recordist, costume maker, designer, lighting operator, publicity manager . . . These jobs are just as important as the actors in bringing the play to life, and making a success of the final product.

There's a lot of effort involved in getting a play ready for performance. It requires a great deal of co-operation from everyone. But at the end of it all, you may find that there's a real BUZZ in it – for both you and your audience.

THE SYMPATHY CARD

Kevin Fegan

THE CHARACTERS

In class 3B:

Daniel, quiet, thoughtful, good with words
Rebecca
Vicky
Mandy
Adam

In class 3A:

Bagsy (Richard Bagworth)
Lloyd
Emma
Lisa
Wayne

The staff:

Mrs Boot, head-teacher
Miss Scales, 3B's form tutor

At the church:

Uncle Bob
The priest

There are non-speaking parts for other members of class 3A and 3B, and for other people at the church.

About this play

Jamie Scott has been killed in an accident. His schoolmates are asked to attend his funeral service, but first they are given the job of writing a sympathy card to Jamie's parents. It's a job that no one wants. After all, what can you say that doesn't sound sloppy or sentimental . . . or false? How do you find the right words to express your feelings about a subject that people would rather not talk about?

Daniel is the one who finally gets stuck with the job, and he finds that it's every bit as difficult as he thought it would be!

SCENE 1

*(Monday morning. Class 3A. Registration time. The teacher is late, and the class are noisy, amusing themselves. **Wayne** has secretly brought his new air-pistol into school.)*

Lisa   Where's all the teachers this morning?

Lloyd   What you got there?

*(**Wayne** attempts to hide his air-pistol but only half-heartedly.)*

Lloyd   Wayne's got a gun!

Bagsy   Hey, let's have a look, Wayne.

*(**Wayne** resists **Bagsy's** attempt to take the pistol off him.)*

Bagsy   Have you got any pellets?

*(**Wayne** pulls out a tin of air pellets. The others gather around. **Wayne** enjoys their attention.)*

Lloyd   You'll get murdered if they catch you with that.

*(**Bagsy** grabs it and points it at the girls.)*

Emma   Bagsy!

Lisa   He's not right in the head. If you were a bird Bagsy, you'd fly backwards.

Bagsy   Hey, we could shoot at the birds out of the window.

Emma   Don't you dare!

Lisa   Put it down, Bagsy.

*(**Lloyd** grabs the air-pistol.)*

Lloyd   Let's have a look.

(The boys gather around the gun, the girls group in an opposite corner.)

SCENE 2

(Class 3B. Registration time. Everyone is unusually quiet.)

Vicky I can't believe it.

Rebecca We walked home together on Friday.

Adam I should have realised.

Mandy What do you mean?

Daniel Adam thinks he's responsible.

Mandy It was an accident, wasn't it?

Vicky I blame his mum and dad.

Rebecca I didn't even say, 'goodbye'. I didn't know I wouldn't be seeing him again.

Mandy Tell us what happened, Adam. Was it an accident?

*(They group around **Adam**.)*

SCENE 3

*(Class 3A. **Bagsy** has turned the class dustbin onto its side and chalked a bullseye target on the bottom of the bin. **Lloyd** is collecting money from those pupils who want a shot at the target.)*

Lloyd Roll up! 10p a go! Whoever hits nearest the bull wins 50 per cent of the takings! Roll up!

Emma Let's sit down, Lisa, before they get us all into trouble.

*(**Lloyd** approaches **Emma** and **Lisa**, using the pistol like a highwayman. **Bagsy** whistles a menacing tune – like one from a 'Clint Eastwood' film.)*

Lloyd Your money or your life, ladies?

Lisa Get lost, Clint!

Emma Lloyd, that's dangerous.

Lloyd Don't be stupid, it's not loaded.

Emma   It could be.

Lloyd   It's not, look.

Emma   Take it away!

Wayne   I've got the pellets, stupid.

Lisa   One of the lads now, are we Wayne? At long last.

Emma   Creep!

*(**Lloyd** and **Bagsy** leave the classroom.)*

Wayne   Where are you going?

Lloyd   We're going to see where the teachers are before we start –
just in case.

Wayne   Don't leave me with this lot.

*(Exit **Lloyd** and **Bagsy**.)*

SCENE 4

*(In the school entrance hall, **Lloyd** and **Bagsy** dive behind a curtain as
Mrs Boot and **Miss Scales** enter the building. **Mrs Boot** looks as
if she has been crying. She dabs her eyes with a handkerchief.)*

Bagsy   Watch out – Bootsy's coming!

(The boys eavesdrop on the teachers' conversation.)

Miss Scales   I do think it would be better coming from you, Mrs
Boot.

*(**Mrs Boot** braces herself and puts away her hanky.
Bagsy peeps through the curtain. **Lloyd** whispers.)*

Lloyd   What can you see, Bagsy?

Bagsy   Ssh!

Mrs Boot   Very well, Anne.

Miss Scales   I hope you don't think worse of me for this. It's just
that . . .

Mrs Boot   It's all right, I understand.

Miss Scales   They don't really prepare you for this sort of thing in College do they?

Mrs Boot   And head-teachers are expected to have a natural flair for it.

Lloyd   What are they on about?

Bagsy   Shut up, will you?

Miss Scales   The class probably know already.

Mrs Boot   They still have to be told.

(The boys are getting more and more curious.)

Bagsy   Told what?

Mrs Boot   Class 3B first. I'll inform the rest of the school in assembly.

Miss Scales   He was such a gentle boy.

Mrs Boot   And a good swimmer, I believe?

Miss Scales   You never expect it with one of your own class . . . not a fatal accident.

Bagsy   Who?

Mrs Boot   Something should be done to make the canal safer.

Lloyd   What?

(The teachers start to walk away.)

Mrs Boot   What was his first name, Anne?

Miss Scales   Jamie. Jamie Scott.

Bagsy   Jamie Scott! Quick!

Lloyd   Where are we going?

Bagsy   3B. Come on, Jamie Scott's dead.

(They run off.)

SCENE 5

*(Class 3B. Enter **Bagsy** and **Lloyd**, excited.)*

Lloyd   We've just heard – is it true?

(The class silence is his reply.)

Bagsy Did he fall in or jump?

(No response. The class seems to have united against 'outsiders'.)

Bagsy Well?

*(**Bagsy** tries to shock them out of their silence.)*

Bagsy I heard he was green when they dragged him out.

Mandy Green?

Rebecca Bagsy!

Adam Get him out of here, will you?

*(**Daniel** tries a sarcastic approach.)*

Daniel That's what I like about you, Bagsy. You're so sensitive!

Bagsy Does it matter? He's dead, isn't he?

Rebecca Don't say that.

Bagsy Why not? It's the truth.

Vicky He's right. We have to face up to it.

Lloyd Mrs Boot's coming! Quick!

*(Enter **Mrs Boot** and **Miss Scales**.)*

Miss Scales Richard Bagworth and Lloyd Jones, what are you boys doing here? Return to Class 3A at once and tell everyone to wait until the class is called to assembly.

Bagsy Yes, Miss Scales.

Lloyd Yes, Miss Scales.

Mrs Boot Thank you, Miss Scales.

*(Exit **Bagsy** and **Lloyd**. **Mrs Boot** faces the class.)*

Mrs Boot Some of you will have heard of the tragic news about Jamie Scott who was sadly taken from us at the weekend. Miss Scales has asked me to come along this morning to support her class through this difficult time. Is there anyone not yet aware of what I am talking about?

(No response.)

Mrs Boot   Fine. I understand from Miss Scales that Jamie was a popular boy and an intelligent pupil. However, it is better, perhaps, not to view his . . . his misfortune as a waste; rather allow it to serve as a lesson to us all about the need for considering personal safety at all times. I have spoken to Miss Scales and we think it would be a good idea for Class 3B to compose a sympathy card signed by all class members, which we will deliver in person with a wreath to Jamie's parents. Naturally, we will buy the wreath from school funds so there will be no need to involve *your* parents. I will, however, be sending them a letter to tell them what we are doing. Miss Scales will help you with the sympathy card. Any questions?

Mandy   Please Mrs Boot, Bagsy – er, Richard Bagworth – wanted to know did Jamie fall in, or did he jump?

Mrs Boot   Really, Amanda, I am shocked by your heartless attitude.

Mandy   Sorry, Mrs Boot.

Mrs Boot   I do not think it is our place to speculate on the exact details of this tragedy.

Mandy   No, Mrs Boot. Sorry, Mrs Boot.

*(**Mrs Boot** goes. The girls comfort **Mandy**.
Miss Scales hands over the sympathy card to **Daniel**.)*

Miss Scales   Daniel, would you take charge of the card?

(She leaves before he has a chance to hand it back.)

Daniel   But, Miss . . . !

SCENE 6

*(Class 3A. **Bagsy** and **Lloyd** have told them about Jamie's death.)*

Lisa   Who was he?

Emma   You know, he always used to hang around with Adam.

Lloyd   You'd better pack this lot away 'cos Mrs Boot will be here any minute.

Lisa What did he look like?

Emma Difficult to describe, really; sort of ordinary.

*(Nobody wants to play with the air-pistol any more, but **Lloyd** teases **Wayne** about it.)*

Lloyd Go on then, Wayne. You start. It's your gun!

Wayne You're not going to tell on me, are you?

Emma There were always rumours he was going out with Rebecca, only she never let on . . . and I don't think he'd dare.

*(**Lisa** realises who they've been talking about.)*

Lisa Oh! You mean Scotty?

Emma That's him, Jamie Scott.

Lisa I never knew his real name.

Bagsy Wouldn't look very good, Wayne, would it: a mystery death in the school and you with a murder weapon?

Emma Stop messing about, Bagsy! This is for real.

Bagsy I didn't know him, did I?

Emma Does that matter? It could just as easily have been someone from this class.

Bagsy Yeah – but it wasn't, was it?

SCENE 7

*(Class 3B. **Mandy** is crying. She is still upset by **Mrs Boot's** telling-off.)*

Rebecca It's all right, Mandy; it's not your fault. Don't cry.

Mandy She made me feel vulgar – like I was staring at a road accident or something.

Vicky She's the insensitive one – talking about him as another 'lesson'; as if he'd been timetabled for this week's discussion.

Rebecca I don't think Mrs Boot meant it like that. You could tell *she'd* been crying – and Miss Scales.

Vicky   The 'old Boot' crying? Never. Miss Scales, I could imagine; but –

Rebecca   Teachers aren't mates; you shouldn't expect them to feel the same way about it.

Mandy   No; but you should be able to talk to them about things.

Daniel   Does it matter?

Mandy   I tell my sister everything.

Daniel   I tell my dog – at least he can't use it against me.

Vicky   You should be able to talk to your mum about everything – I do.

Adam   Huh! That's a joke for a start.

Vicky   Well, your dad then.

Adam   That's even more of a joke.

Rebecca   I think that's what friends are for.

Adam   I wish they weren't.

Daniel   It's up to us – as friends – to write this sympathy card.

Mandy   What should we write?

Vicky   Who's the card for anyway? Jamie won't be able to read it, will he?

Rebecca   It's for his mum and dad, stupid.

Adam   They don't deserve a card.

Vicky   I agree.

Mandy   Why not?

Adam   They didn't care about him.

Rebecca   How do you know?

Adam   He told me: he hated them.

Daniel   Everyone says that about their parents sometimes.

Adam   He meant it.

Mandy   Why? What did they do to him?

Adam   They used him.

Mandy   What do you mean?

Adam   As a weapon.

Rebecca   They still loved him.

Adam   He asked me if he could come and stay at my house the night before it happened. I said 'no' because I daren't ask my mum. He begged me; but I was in my mum's bad books for painting my room. I daren't ask her. I didn't know he was thinking of doing away with himself.

Rebecca   We don't know if that's what happened.

Daniel   Have you told the police?

Adam   They haven't asked.

Mandy   Did Jamie tell you why he wanted to stay?

Adam   He said he couldn't stand them fighting.

Daniel   We still have to write this card.

Adam   *I* don't.

Rebecca   They'll be heartbroken. I know they will.

Mandy   More than heartbroken, I should imagine.

Rebecca   You didn't know them, Adam. I've been to his house quite a few times.

(*Vicky starts to tease* **Rebecca**.)

Vicky   It's all coming out now.

Rebecca   It wasn't like that. We were friends. We didn't want you lot jumping to conclusions.

Vicky   What makes you think we'd be interested?

(**Rebecca** *ignores her.*)

Rebecca   His dad is lovely. His mum's a bit moody; but they loved him, you could tell.

Daniel Look, it's not our place to judge his parents. What are we going to write?

Mandy With sympathy.

Rebecca With love.

Vicky Without slush.

Mandy It's not slush to show your feelings.

Vicky You should know.

Rebecca Come on then – what do you suggest?

Vicky Something straightforward and truthful like 'Sorry to hear your son is dead'.

Mandy We can't write that.

Daniel I don't think she means it.

Vicky I do.

Daniel We have to be more sensitive about how we say it.

Rebecca It's not easy to think of the right words, is it?

Mandy What about a little verse?

Vicky 'Roses are red, violets are blue,
Jamie is dead and –'

Rebecca '– one day . . . with luck . . . you will be too.'

Mandy Only you won't get a card.

Vicky Charming.

Daniel Can we be serious about this, please?

Rebecca You write it, Daniel.

Mandy We'll all sign it.

Adam
Rebecca } (*together*) Yes.
Mandy

Daniel No, that's not fair.

Vicky Go on, Danny, you're best at that sort of thing.

Daniel   Best at what?

Vicky   You know, English.

Daniel   Being good at English isn't the most appropriate qualification for writing this.

Vicky   See: you know all the big words.

Rebecca   Whatever you say is bound to read better than what any of us could write.

Daniel   But I hardly knew him. It would sound false. You should write it, Becky.

Rebecca   I couldn't face it.

Daniel   Or you, Adam?

Adam   It's harder if you knew him.

*(Enter **Miss Scales**.)*

Miss Scales   How are you getting on?

Vicky   Daniel's going to write it for us, Miss.

Daniel   I never said!

Miss Scales   Thank you, Daniel. That's very brave of you.

Daniel   Miss, they'll only make sarcky comments about it.

Miss Scales   Nonsense. You won't, will you class?

All   No, Miss.

Daniel   I won't have to read it out at the church, will I?

Miss Scales   No.

Daniel   And no one else will read it out, will they?

Miss Scales   Of course not, no.

Daniel   I still don't know what to write.

Miss Scales   I'm sure you'll manage, Daniel.
   Now then, class, I have a letter here for your parents.

*(**Miss Scales** hands out the letters. They leave **Daniel** alone to work on the card.)*

Daniel   How can I put it?
  I usually like writing. There's supposed to be a word for
  everything, if you can find it. But sometimes – I think – words
  can fail you . . .

(He sits there, trying hard to find the right words.)

SCENE 8

(A few days later, outside the school. A coach arrives to take classes 3B and 3A to the church for Jamie's funeral. Class 3A boards the coach first.)

Lisa   Me first, I'm freezing.

Lloyd   No need to push.

Bagsy   I don't see why we have to go – he wasn't even in our class.

Emma   Mrs Boot says both third-year classes should go 'as a mark of respect'.

Wayne   Save the back seat.

Lloyd   Respect for what?

Bagsy   Shouldn't complain, I suppose: it's a day out of school.

Emma   I don't know how you can joke about it?

Bagsy   You're so serious, you. Nobody's going to think any better of you for moping around with a face like you've missed the last bus.

Wayne   Bags I sit next to the window.

Emma   You can't recognise genuine grief.

Bagsy   Jamie wouldn't want us to be miserable, would he?

(Class 3B boards the coach.)

Mandy   Back seat's gone.

Vicky   Who invited *them*? I don't know why they're going?

Mandy   My mum says I shouldn't be going to a funeral at my age. It's not right.

Daniel   Mrs Boot said in her letter that anyone who didn't want their child to attend the service should write to her so alternative arrangements could be made.

Adam   Who's holding us up? Come on.

Vicky   Sit at the front with the teachers, you, if you want to organise.

Adam   That's Daniel's place, isn't it?

*(**Daniel** says nothing but is upset by the remark.)*

Mandy   Yea, well my mum says she's too busy to write letters. Anyway, she always has to ask me to check her spelling.

(The coach pulls away.)

Bagsy   Hurrah!

*(**Adam** finds an empty seat next to **Rebecca**.)*

Adam   I suppose I'll have to sit with you.

*(**Miss Scales** calls out from the front of the coach.)*

Miss Scales   Has everyone found a seat? Richard Bagworth, stop calling out of the window.

(He shouts back.)

Bagsy   I wasn't, miss. I was just throwing this sweet-wrapper out.

Miss Scales   Honestly!! Just close the window, will you?

Bagsy   Yes, miss.

*(**Rebecca** speaks to **Adam**.)*

Rebecca   I'm frightened.

Adam   Me too.

Rebecca   Have you ever been before? To a funeral, I mean.

*(**Vicky** leans over the seat and interrupts.)*

Vicky   I have. To my gran's. Only that was a cremation. And I was only about six. It was horrible.

Adam   We're not actually going to the cemetery.

Mandy Will 'he' be there?

Adam Jamie?

Mandy Yes.

Adam 'Course he will, you idiot.

Vicky Star of the show.

Rebecca Stop it.

Adam He'll be laid out in the church.

Mandy We won't have to look at him, will we? I couldn't bear it.

Adam The lid will be on the coffin, if that's what you mean.

Mandy Yea, but he's inside, isn't he?

Daniel It would be more scary if he wasn't.

Vicky You think they would have invented a better system by now, don't you?

Daniel They have – freezing them.

Rebecca Adam. Swap seats, I want to be near the heater.

Adam It's not worth it, we're there now.

Vicky That's disgusting, Daniel.

Daniel And costly.

Mandy I don't see the point?

Vicky Nobody can live forever.

*(**Bagsy** pushes his way down the coach.)*

Bagsy I dunno; the 'old Boot' is doing all right. Excuse me, ladies.

Adam It's a horrible thought: knowing you're going to die some day.

(The coach stops.)

Rebecca Don't.

Adam Sorry.

(They leave the coach and file into the church.)

SCENE 9

*(In church. The **Priest** is speaking.)*

Priest   . . . It is especially difficult at this time to understand why God allows such tragedies to befall our families. It is only right and proper to allow ourselves time to grieve. However, I am sure Jamie would want us all to think of the future and to ways in which we might improve the value of our own short stay on earth. I urge you to draw on the strength of your faith in the knowledge that Jamie has truly gone to a better place.

Our thoughts go out to Jamie's parents, his relatives and his school-friends, many of whom are here today.

If the staff and pupils of the school would care to pay their last respects and lay their wreaths.

Mrs Boot   Single file out of the pews, children. Line up behind Daniel – do you have the wreath and the card, Daniel?

*(**Daniel** is very frightened.)*

Daniel   Yes, Mrs Boot.

Mrs Boot   Quickly and quietly, please. Past the coffin and assemble in the churchyard.

(The pupils file out in total silence.)

*(**Miss Scales** whispers to her.)*

Miss Scales   I've never seen them so subdued.

Mrs Boot   It must be a terrible shock for them. I hope we're doing the right thing, bringing them to church.

Miss Scales   We were asked. It's probably better than letting their imaginations run riot. In the long term I'm sure it will help them to get over it.

Mrs Boot   I think we can expect a delayed reaction when their shock wears off.

Miss Scales   One or two of them seem particularly upset by it. We'll have to keep an eye on them.

Mrs Boot   I suppose we had better follow. I think the family are waiting for the bearers.

Miss Scales   His parents look as if they've been through it.

Mrs Boot   I don't suppose they've slept much since it happened.

Miss Scales   No matter what your kids do, you always blame yourself as a parent.

Mrs Boot   And as a Teacher.

(*A man comes over to talk to them.*)

Uncle Bob   Excuse me. Mrs Boot?

Mrs Boot   Yes?

Uncle Bob   I'm Jamie's Uncle Robert – Bob. Jamie's parents – have asked me to thank you and the school for coming along this morning. They'd have thanked you themselves, only . . . I'm sure you understand?

Mrs Boot   Of course. It must have been an awful shock for them.

Uncle Bob   I thought the Priest did us a wonderful service. He spoke very well.

Mrs Boot   Quite. Have you met Miss Scales – Jamie's Form Teacher?

Uncle Bob   How-do-you-do.

Miss Scales   Hello. Thanks very much for reassuring us. We really were a little uncertain about our response, even though Mr and Mrs Scott did ask us to attend.

(**Mrs Boot** *is slightly annoyed and embarrassed at* **Miss Scales** *revealing the nature of their private conversation.*)

Mrs Boot   Were we uncertain? No, I don't think so, Miss Scales.

Uncle Bob   I'm sure Jamie would be pleased to know his schoolmates felt so much about him.

(**Mrs Boot** *exaggerates.*)

Mrs Boot   Oh yes, he was a very popular boy.

Miss Scales   The unfortunate experience does seem to have brought them closer together.

Uncle Bob   I'd like to have a word with them, if I may?

Mrs Boot   They are waiting outside for the coach. You'll have to be quick.

(She leads the way. They exit from the church and group on the steps. The pupils are waiting for them.)

Mrs Boot   Classes 3A and 3B: would you gather around the steps, please. Thank you. This is Jamie's Uncle Robert.

(There are awkward smiles all around.)

Mrs Boot   He has something to say to you.

Uncle Bob   Oh, right. Yes, erm . . . well, I don't quite know how to put this. I suppose I wanted to thank you all for   , supporting this – no, that's not right. I'm not much good with words; but I know if our Jamie was here today . . . oh dear . . . I mean . . . well I know our Jamie would have wanted to thank you. And his mum and dad especially appreciate the wreath and the card.

*(He turns to **Daniel**.)*

Uncle Bob   This young lad here did a marvellous job laying the wreath and the card – I understand you composed the message yourself? I'd like to read it out, if I may. It's so appropriate.

*(**Daniel** bursts into tears and runs on to the coach. Everyone is shocked, especially **Uncle Bob**. He apologises to **Mrs Boot**.)*

Uncle Bob   Oh dear, I am sorry, I didn't mean to –

Miss Scales   I'll see to him.

*(**Miss Scales** goes to the coach.)*

Mrs Boot   Would you board the coach immediately, please – Class 3B first.

Uncle Bob   I am sorry, Mrs – Head-teacher.

*(**Mrs Boot** wants to make a quick exit.)*

Mrs Boot   Not to worry. We really must be getting back to school. Do convey our sympathies once again to Mr and Mrs Scott.

*(**Mrs Boot** hurries the pupils towards the coach. Meanwhile . . . on the front seat of the coach **Miss Scales** talks to **Daniel**.)*

Miss Scales Daniel?

Daniel Go away. Leave me alone.

Miss Scales It's perfectly natural to cry, Daniel, if that's what you're worried about?

Daniel Don't ask me to do that ever again.

Miss Scales What?

Daniel I'm fourteen, miss. And I do still cry. And it's not fair to load me up with too many responsibilities.

Miss Scales You mean, the card and the wreath and everything?

Daniel Yes!

Miss Scales You should have said. I could have helped you. I didn't realise. I thought you enjoyed being the responsible one.

Daniel So does the rest of the class.

(He starts to mimic the others.)

Daniel 'You do it, Daniel, you're good with words. Good old Daniel, he can organise us.'

Miss Scales I'm sorry.

Daniel So am I. Jamie is dead and I'm expected to make it all right with words –

Miss Scales No one expects you to –

Daniel . . . when the adults don't even know what to say or how to say it. It's not fair.

Miss Scales You're right. It's not fair. It's too much to ask of anyone. I only wish there was some way round it. You can't say what you feel and you can't feel what you say. Come on, Daniel, we'll grab the back seat before the others get on.

*(He mimics something **Vicky** said earlier.)*

Daniel 'Sit at the front with the teachers if you want to organise.'

Miss Scales Pardon?

Daniel Nothing, miss.

(They move to the back seat. The others board.)

Mandy Better now, Daniel?

Vicky Phew! I'm glad that's over with – especially Uncle Bob.

(Everyone starts to look for a seat. There's not much talking.)

Miss Scales You're not saying much, Bagsy, not like you?

Bagsy No, miss.

*(**Lloyd** grabs **Wayne** as he goes past.)*

Lloyd You can sit next to me if you like.

Wayne Thanks.

Lloyd And don't bring your air-pistol to school again.

Wayne I won't.

Lloyd You can muck in with us without having to bribe us, you know?

Wayne Sorry.

*(**Rebecca** sits next to **Adam**.)*

Rebecca We never got to speak to his mum and dad.

Adam I don't need to. I know now it must have been an accident.

Rebecca So you can stop blaming yourself?

Adam Thanks, Rebecca. You were right.

Rebecca I'll miss Jamie.

Adam Me too.

Talking Points

(For discussion in small groups, write each 'Talking Point' on a separate piece of card.)

1. Was Mrs Boot right to take the third years to Jamie's funeral?

2. Should teachers inform pupils about a classmate's death or should they let them find out in other ways?

3. Why do the two classes react so differently to Jamie's death?

4. Why does Adam think he's partly to blame for Jamie's death?

5. Nobody in 3B wants to take responsibility for writing the sympathy card. Why is it such a difficult task?

6. Why does Bagsy react to the news of Jamie's death in the way he does?

7. Why is Daniel so upset by Uncle Bob's remarks in the church?

8. Do you think that anyone in 3A or 3B is changed by the experience of attending Jamie's funeral?

Investigations

1. What does Daniel write in the sympathy card to Jamie's parents? He didn't know him very well, so it's going to sound false if he talks of him as a close friend.

   The others advise him that the message should be written 'with sympathy . . . with love . . . without slush'. Someone also suggests that there should be a little verse.

   Daniel knows it's going to be difficult to find the right words, but he finally manages to come up with something that Jamie's family really appreciates.

   Write your version of the sympathy card – by yourself or with a partner.

2. Many of us find it difficult to talk to people who are mourning the death of someone close to them. Sometimes we try to avoid meeting them. If we do meet them – or write to them – we often use words that don't mention the subject in a straightforward way. Mrs Boot does this when she tells 3B the news about Jamie. She doesn't say 'Jamie is dead'; instead, she says that Jamie has been 'sadly taken from us'. She is using what's called a 'euphemism'. At other points in the play, you will find examples of people talking in this way. They are usually trying to avoid using the word 'death', and they're doing it because they say they don't want to cause more distress to the people they're talking to.

Can you think of some other situations where people try to find less upsetting words and expressions to soften or disguise the truth? Either by yourself, or with a partner, list the situations you have in mind, with examples of the 'euphemisms' people use in those situations.

Situations	Euphemism
Stealing	'borrowing', 'half-inching'
Lying	'being economical with the truth'

3. The school sent every parent a letter explaining why forms 3A and 3B were being taken to the funeral (pp. 15 and 20).

What reasons do you think Mrs Boot would give to parents?

She also gave parents the right to ask for their children not to go. On your own, or with a partner, write the letter that Mrs Boot sent the parents.

Read out your letter to the rest of the class.

Put yourself in the place of a parent. Would you want your children to go to the funeral or not?

4. To mark the first anniversary of Jamie's death, his parents have given the school some money to be spent on a 'Jamie Scott Prize'. The prize will be awarded each year. All the people in Jamie's class have been asked to say what they think the prize should be given for. Should it reward good work, house activities, sporting achievements . . . etc? Everybody has to write down at least three suggestions in order of importance and give reasons for their choices. What would you write?

Read out your ideas to the rest of the class and see which suggestion seems to be the most popular. Then write a short letter to Jamie's parents telling them what the class has decided – and why. But remember this could be an upsetting time of year for them.

5. It's not easy to give someone bad news. For example, Miss Scales doesn't want to tell 3B about Jamie's death. 'They don't really prepare you for this sort of thing in College . . .' she tells Mrs Boot.

In pairs, act out a situation in which one of you has to break bad news to the other. It needn't be anything as dramatic or upsetting as somebody's death, but it could be news that will cause a lot of disappointment or sadness.

Before you start the conversation, write out a list together of three or four situations where you hear some bad news. Perhaps a friend is going to move away, or a trip you've looked forward to is cancelled, or a pet is involved in an accident . . . You decide. When you've made your list put it away. Choose who will break the bad news first. That person chooses one of the situations from the list, but doesn't say which one. How will you begin to break the news? Will you come straight out with it . . . or will you talk about other matters first? Will you take on a very sympathetic tone of voice . . . or be very casual and matter of fact? What will you say to overcome your partner's disappointment?

When you've tried out the first situation, swap over and let the other person secretly choose another topic on the list. How will you break the news about this one?

Tell the rest of the class how you did? Were you pleased with the way you managed to break the news? How did you do it?

6. Daniel is very upset at the end of the play, but the only person to comfort him is Miss Scales. He's upset by what he's been asked to do, and he feels that he's handled everything very badly by bursting into tears. It would be good if he had some friends to help him through this bad time.

If he came to you — as his friends — what would you say to him to make him feel better?

Work in groups of three or four, with one of you as Daniel. Prepare a scene to show how you would try to help him.

Let the others watch, and listen to their comments about the way you handled the situation.

Did they think that you handled it tactfully and sympathetically?

Did they like the advice you gave?

Now show the scene again. This time let the class give *you* advice on how to deal with Daniel by interrupting the action, and telling you what to do and say.

7. At the funeral service the priest says, '. . . I am sure Jamie would want us all to think of the future and to ways in which we might improve the value of our own short stay here on earth.'

In small groups, work out a 'still photograph' in which you take on the part of one of the third years at the funeral service. Arrange yourselves in the way you think that the group might be sitting, and then speak your thoughts one after the other.

You may need to look back through the play to check up on how your character thinks and speaks, and what they feel about Jamie's death. You could have more than one person playing the same character, though it might be less confusing to your audience if you don't!

Show your 'photograph' to the others. Let them try to identify which character you're playing.

8. You are asked to make a film or video version of *The Sympathy Card*. Design what you think the sets would look like for each of the scenes.

Your drawings can be as simple or as detailed as you want. You'll need to have sketches for each of the following settings:

> *a classroom* (which could be the same for 3A and 3B, but with different wall displays);
> *the school entrance hall* (with a curtain for Bagsy and Lloyd to hide behind);
> *the inside of a coach*;
> *the inside of the church*;
> *the churchyard.*

Label your designs and point out any special features that you think are important.

THE BIRTHDAY PRESENT

Janys Chambers

THE CHARACTERS

The play concerns two main families and their friends.

The Summers family:

Edie (Edith) Summers
Lionel Summers
Emily, their youngest daughter, at college
Fran, their eldest daughter, living and working in Cornwall

Edie's friends:

Marje
Mave
Yazmine

Emily's friends:

Heather
Maya

The Clark family:

Jo Clark
Michael Clark
Hannah, who first appears at the age of 9, and later at the age of 15

Other characters:

James, Hannah's boyfriend
A woman attendant at the Turkish baths
Mr Mahal, a social worker
A woman on the beach
A small boy on the beach

About this play

This play is a bit like a jigsaw puzzle. You have to fit the pieces together to make a complete picture. As you read through, we hope that the pieces will begin to fit together for you, and that the picture will slowly become clearer.

So, you won't find a description of the story here, because that would spoil the mystery. All you need to know before you begin reading is that the play is divided intò ten scenes. Scene 1 is set in March, Scene 2 in April, Scene 3 in May. So the play continues month by month and ends with Scene 10 set in December. But now for the catch. We move backwards and forwards in time throughout the play. So the March scene, for example, is March 1973, the April scene, April 1983. Curious? Then read on.

SCENE 1 MARCH 1973

(Nottingham. The rest-room in the Turkish baths. Three women arrive, **Mave, Edie** *and* **Yazmine**. *They regularly spend their afternoons relaxing here when they are not working. Their friend,* **Marje**, *who hasn't arrived yet, has just retired from work.*
The women head for four rest-beds.)

Mave   Here, quick, look! Four beds in a row!

Edie   Oh, that's good. Now put some things on that one for Marje.

Mave   You'd think now she was a lady of leisure she'd be here first, getting the beds for us.

(They start to take their clothes off.)

Edie   Oh, that's better. Ruddy bra's supposed to lift and separate, not chop me in two.

Yazmine   I'm hungry.

Edie   You have to sweat a bit of weight off first, before you can start eating!

Mave   Look, I've brought us some nice grapes for later.

(They put on their dressing-gowns, sit on the beds and start arranging their things on the bedside tables. **Yazmine** *calls an attendant.)*

34   **Yazmine**   Excuse me!

Attendant What can I get for you?

Yazmine Can I order a salad sandwich on brown bread?

Edie Well, at least it's healthy.

Yazmine And a Kit-Kat.

Edie Oh!

Yazmine And a pot of tea for three.

*(**Marje** comes into the rest-room.)*

Mave There's Marje!

Yazmine Four.

Edie We're ordering you some tea, Marje.

Attendant I'll bring it in after you've been in the steam room, shall I?

*(**Mave** nods. The **attendant** goes. **Marge** gets undressed.)*

Mave What's it like then, Marje, being at home all the time?

Marje Well, I've missed you lot. Haven't missed work though.

Mave She could spend every day in here now!

Edie Don't be daft, she'd end up looking like a prune.

Yazmine Can I have a grape?

(They pass the grapes around.)

Marje Edie, how's your Emily doing up at that college? Still doing well is she?

Edie Like a house on fire. Getting really good marks, she is. The tutors are dead pleased with her.

Marje You know you asked me to make something for her, a long time ago? Well, I haven't just been twiddling my thumbs all week. I've finished it.

*(She gets an object wrapped in white tissue paper out of her bag. She unwraps it carefully. It's a very large, very fine white shawl with an intricate pattern, hand-crocheted – a beautiful piece of work. There is silence until, after a while, **Edie** speaks.)*

Edie   It's beautiful. Isn't it?

Mave   It's lovely.

Yazmine   You *are* clever.

Mave   Emily will like that.

Edie   She'll love it.

Marje   They're very fashionable these shawls, you know, with the students. They wear them with these maxi-skirts.

Edie   It's her twenty-first birthday in May. I'll give it her then.

Marje   Will she be home for it?

Edie   Just for that weekend. Lionel's going to make her a special cake.

(*She wraps the shawl round her instead of the dressing-gown, and parades up and down the Turkish bath.*)

Edie   Twiggy Summers!

(*The women laugh. The **attendant** comes back.*)

Yazmine   She's naked as a new-born babe under there.

Mave   I thought you wore them with a maxi-skirt, not your birthday suit.

Attendant   Tea's nearly ready, ladies!

Yazmine   Come on.

(*They reach for towels ready to go over to the steam room.*)

Edie   It *is* lovely, Marje, just right for her birthday.

Marje   Yes, I think she'll like it . . .

(*They go off into the steam room.*)

SCENE 2   APRIL 1983

(*Frampton-on-Severn in Gloucestershire.*
*The village green where a maypole is being erected. A woman, **Jo**, watches; nearby a man, **Michael**, and a small girl, **Hannah**, are having a whispered conversation.*)

Michael   Yes. I think she'll like it . . .

Hannah You've got it? Where is it? Show me!

(*Michael laughs.*)

Michael All right, all right, come further over here then, where she can't see.

(*Michael gets an object wrapped in white tissue paper out of his pocket.*)

Hannah Show me, show me!

Michael All right, I'm unwrapping it as fast as I can.

(*He unwraps the object carefully. It is a large black brooch with a word picked out on it in white pearls.*)

Michael There!

Hannah It's beautiful. Isn't it?

Michael It's lovely. I went to the shop this morning and it was still in the window. The woman remembered you looking.

Hannah How old is it?

Michael It's Victorian, I think. Maybe a hundred years old.

(*Jo calls to them.*)

Jo Aren't we lucky with this sunshine?

Hannah Quick, hide it!

Michael Yes!

Jo Hope it's like this tomorrow!

Michael Yes!

(*He whispers to Hannah.*)

Michael It's all right, she's stopped looking. The black stuff's called jet.

Hannah Are those real pearls?

Michael I shouldn't think so. Well, I don't know. Maybe they are. Seed pearls I think they're called.

Hannah How much was it?

Michael A lot more than your pocket money, I'm afraid.

Hannah   Oh.

Michael   Don't worry. I'll put a bit towards it. It would have been silly not to get it when it's *such* a good present. You can tell her you spotted it all by yourself.

(*Hannah* starts to spell out the letters on the brooch.)

Hannah   M – O –

Michael   Quick, she's coming!

(*Jo walks towards them.* **Hannah** *wraps up the brooch and conceals it in her palm.*)

Michael   Now remember, don't go telling what it is.

Jo   You two don't seem very interested in the maypole going up! It probably hasn't been seen in this village for about a hundred years. Well, fifty anyway.

Hannah   I've got you a birthday present.

Michael   Hannah!

Hannah   But I'm not going to tell you what it is.

Jo   Oh, a secret!

Hannah   Yes!

Michael   *Yes!*

Hannah   And it's not a necklace!

Jo   Oh?

Hannah   Or a bracelet!

Michael   Hannah!

Hannah   Or earrings.

Jo   Well, I'm sure I'll love it, whatever it is.

(*Hannah* skips about with the brooch tight in her hand. **Michael** and **Jo** laugh.)

Jo   Come on then, come and have a proper look at this maypole.

Michael   You should save all that skipping about for the dancing tomorrow. You won't have any energy left.

Hannah   Yes I will, yes I will.

Jo   Yes, she will.

Hannah   My class is doing two dances!

Michael   And then, the next day, it's somebody's birthday.

*(**Hannah** whispers to **Michael**.)*

Hannah   I can't wait to give it her.

SCENE 3   MAY 1973

*(**Edie** and **Lionel's** house in Nottingham.
Emily has just come home from College. She's upstairs. **Edie** whispers to
Lionel.)*

Edie   I can't wait to give it her.

Lionel   Well, when are you going to do it, before or after tea?

Edie   Before.

Lionel   I'll put it back on the chair then, with the other things.

Edie   She likes to do cards first off.

Lionel   They're on her plate.

Edie   Did you get the one from Fran?

Lionel   Yes.

Edie   It was behind the clock?

*(**Lionel** sighs.)*

Lionel   Yes.

Edie   Hers has got a key on it too, I could feel it.

Lionel   Like a baby you are.

Edie   Oh yes! Hark who's talking! Who's spent nearly all week
making her a fancy birthday cake?

*(They look at the cake on the table. It's shaped into numbers, a two and a
one, is enthusiastically iced, and has twenty-one candles on it.)*

Edie   It *is* nice, Lionel. We should cover it up so she doesn't see it till we're ready.

Lionel   Where is she anyway?

Edie   Still in the bathroom.

Lionel   What is she finding to do in there all this time?

Edie   Now then Lionel, don't start.

Lionel   Just like Fran used to be; hours staring at herself in the mirror and worrying about her figure.

Edie   Lionel!

Lionel   Didn't think Emily worried. She's as skinny as a rake that one. Shall I put the kettle on?

Edie   I think she's looking a bit peaky.

Lionel   All that studying. No need really. Got brains our Em, always has had.

Edie   Quick, she's coming!

(They cover the cake. **Emily** *comes into the kitchen.)*

Edie   ⎤ *(together)*   Happy birthday to you, happy birthday to
Lionel ⎦   you, happy birthday dear Emily, happy birthday to you!

Edie   Twenty-one today, twenty-one today, I've got the key of the door, never been twenty-one before. Happy birthday, Emily!

*(**Emily** is embarrassed.)*

Emily   Thank you!

Lionel   Twenty-one eh! Well, you're an adult now. I know some people think you are earlier – but I'm a bit old-fashioned – *I* think this is when it starts. Your life starts here, Em. And I hope it's a very happy one.

Edie   Lionel, stop making a speech, you're making her go all pink!

Lionel   Well, she deserves it! You've got everything going for you Em, doing so well at College and everything. It's been a struggle for Mum and me, but it's been worth it.

Edie Oh, Lionel, that's enough, get the kettle on!

*(She speaks to **Emily**.)*

Edie Just sit down, love, and open your cards. It *is* nice to see you.

Emily It's nice to be home.

*(**Emily** starts opening the cards.)*

Edie Read them out.

Emily 'Happy birthday with love from Nanna.'

Edie That's nice.

Emily This one's from you.

Edie Yes. See, it's got a key on it.

Emily 'We can't believe our baby . . . our baby's all grown up. Happy 21st. Love as always, Mum and Dad.'

Lionel It's true, it doesn't seem a minute since you were in your pram. You were a funny little . . .

Emily Can I have some tea, Dad?

*(**Lionel** hands out the cups of tea. **Emily** goes on opening her cards.)*

Lionel Here you are. Mum, cup of tea. Cup of tea, Em.

Emily 'With lots of love from Fran'.

Edie Told you it was a key on Fran's as well, Lionel.

Emily 'See you soon I hope'.

Edie Look, Lionel!

Emily 'With best wishes on your 21st, Emily, from the girls at Raleigh.'

Edie The girls at work, Lionel! Ah, isn't that nice of them?

Emily 'To Emily, have a happy day, hope you like your present, Marje.'

Edie That's nice, and another key, look!

Emily What's she mean, Mum? Does she know what you've got me?

(*Edie* reaches to her chair and hands over the package.)

Edie Here you are, Em. Yes, she knows. I hope you like it. And Dad's got a little surprise for you, under the tea-towel.

(*Lionel* whisks the cloth off the cake, a bit like a conjuror. *Emily* stares at it.)

Emily You made it.

Edie He's worked on it all week, icing it and everything. Hardly touched his pigeons.

Lionel The 'one's' a bit small compared to the 'two'.

Edie We'll light the candles later. Go on, open the present. Happy Birthday, Em. We're very proud of you, like Dad says.

(*Emily* says nothing. Slowly she unwraps the present. She takes out the shawl.)

Edie Do you like it? I thought you could wear it with your long skirts, at all your college parties. White'll go with all your pretty dresses. Nice and cool too, now that summer's coming.

(*Emily* still says nothing.)

Edie It's hand-made, Marje made it. Took her months. See how fine it is? Like a baby shawl.

(*Emily* bursts into tears.)

Edie Emily! Emily! Don't cry! What's the matter?

Emily Look, will you sit down, I've got something to tell you.

SCENE 4 JUNE 1989

(*Michael* and *Jo Clark's* cottage at Frampton-on-Severn.
Jo is putting up some shelves. She is with *Hannah*. *Hannah* is now fifteen.)

Hannah Look, will you sit down, I've got something to tell you.

Jo Just let me finish drilling this hole.

Hannah No, please stop, there's something I want to talk to you about.

Jo All right, Hannah, there's no need to shout at me.

Hannah I'm sorry. You're always so busy. I've only noticed since I wanted to talk to you. You never stop.

Jo I'm sorry. I just wanted to get these shelves up in your room. They are for you, you know.

Hannah I know. I know they're for me. I just wish you'd talk to me sometimes.

Jo Well, I'm listening now.

(**Hannah** *doesn't speak.*)

Jo Well, what is it? Come on Hannah. Oh for goodness' sake, I've stopped what I was doing, what do you want?

Hannah It's not easy.

Jo You're not in trouble?

Hannah I've spoken to Dad already.

Jo You have. Oh God, you *are* in trouble. What is it? You aren't pregnant, are you?

Hannah Oh Mum, no! Look, it's just hard to say it.

Jo But not to your dad.

Hannah It's harder to say it to you. I wanted him to talk to you really, but he said I should do it myself and then he'd talk to you later.

Jo Am I so hard to talk to?

Hannah No. I just thought you might be more upset. And it's not about you. It's about me really. There's something I've decided I want to do. You said I might one day.

Jo Oh?

Hannah I want to find out. I want to know.

Jo Go on.

Hannah Look, it's nothing to do with you. You're both brilliant. It's me.

Jo   It's all right, Hannah. Don't worry. Go on.

Hannah   I just don't want to upset everybody . . .

SCENE 5   JULY 1973

*(The bedroom of a friend of **Emily's** called **Heather**.*
*She and **Maya**, another friend, are comforting **Emily**.)*

Emily   I just don't want to upset everybody . . .

Heather   Don't worry about us. It's what friends are for.

Emily   I just seem to start crying every five minutes. And then Mum cries with me. It's awful.

Heather   What about your dad?

Emily   He doesn't say much. But I've never seen him look so worried. And they know everyone will know soon. All their friends.

(She starts to cry.)

Emily   And they were so proud of me. I've made such a mess of everything.

Heather   No, you haven't. It'll be all right. Oh God, let's turn that Simon and Garfunkel record off. It's driving me nuts.

(She reaches out and switches off the record player.)

Maya   Look, things *are* better than they were. It's all sorted out for you to go back later to College, isn't it?

Emily   Yes.

Maya   And at least you know *what* you're going to do now. Don't you?

Emily   You know, sometimes I've thought of going away. Right away, where nobody knows me. No one from College, no one from home. Where Mum wouldn't see me every day and get upset. Not speak to anyone. And then come back when it's all over. But I can't think of anywhere.

Maya   Your mum would really worry then.

Emily   But I can't stay here. It's awful! I can't bear it.

*(She is very upset. **Heather** hugs her.)*

Heather   Oh Em. I'll make us some more coffee.

(She goes.)

Maya   What about Fran?

Emily   Fran?

Maya   She knows, doesn't she?

Emily   Mum told her.

Maya   And doesn't she live miles away?

Emily   In Cornwall.

Maya   Well, why don't you go and stay with her? Your mum wouldn't worry if you were with her. You know . . . family, older sister to look after you . . . all that stuff.

Emily   I don't know.

Heather   Here you are, coffee. And some wine left over from the last party!

Emily   She might not want me, great soggy mess that I am.

Maya   You could ask. Heather, we're talking about Em going to stay with Fran, what d'you think?

Heather   In Cornwall? Great idea.

Emily   We don't really know each other very well. We're years apart . . .

Heather   How many is it?

Emily   Eighteen.

SCENE 6   AUGUST 1989

*(The Social Services building in Gloucester.
A small office belonging to **Mr Mahal**, a Social Services worker.)*

Hannah   Eighteen?

Mr Mahal   That's right.

45

Hannah   But that's ages away. I'm only fifteen.

Mr Mahal   The law says you have to be an adult.

Hannah   I'm an adult now.

Mr Mahal   Legally.

Hannah   But it's ages!

Mr Mahal   It could be worse. Once, you weren't an adult till you were twenty-one.

Hannah   But my parents give their consent.

Mr Mahal   I know. It doesn't make any difference. It's the law.

Hannah   I want to know. I've decided.

Mr Mahal   Look. I know it's hard. But think – this is probably one of the biggest decisions you'll make in your whole life, if not *the* biggest. This gives you extra time to think.

Hannah   Time to think! Three years? Look, I've thought!

Mr Mahal   You may *think* you have.

Hannah   Stop treating me like a child!

Mr Mahal   I'm sorry. I don't mean to. I'm sure you have thought. It's just this is a very big thing. It could change your whole life. It could change you. Your family. And not necessarily in the way you think, either.

(He pauses.)

Mr Mahal   I'm only saying the same things I say to everyone . . . to people who're eighteen and even much older. We'll have to say them again to you when you *are* eighteen, if you still want to go ahead. Everyone has to have counselling.

*(**Hannah** doesn't speak.)*

Mr Mahal   Look, they may not even be alive. Have you thought of that, of how you'd feel?

*(**Hannah** goes very still.)*

Mr Mahal   Or they may be living in some way that you don't like; a way that shocks you.

*(Still **Hannah** says nothing.)*

Mr Mahal   Or *they* may not want to know you, or have anything to do with you.

Hannah   They would!

Mr Mahal   Maybe. They might want too *much*. Do you know what I mean by that? How would your parents feel then? Jo and Michael? Do you see?

Hannah   Yes. A bit. I still think it's wrong. I'm fifteen. And I'm not stupid.

Mr Mahal   Clearly.

Hannah   I don't feel as though I know who I am any more!

SCENE 7   SEPTEMBER 1973

(A beach in Cornwall.
***Emily** and her sister **Fran** are walking along the sands. A **woman** and a small **boy** are playing nearby.)*

Emily   I don't feel as though I know who I am any more!

Fran   You'll find yourself again.

Emily   I'm getting big now. People stand up for me on the bus.

*(The **boy** calls out to his **mother**.)*

Boy   Mum!

Woman   Come on then! Let's make a castle!

Emily   I just go red.

*(**Fran** looks at the small **boy** and laughs.)*

Fran   Look at that little boy!

Emily   Fran, sometimes I want to keep it.

Fran   I know.

Emily   But I can't. I've only just started College. I want to go on.

Woman   That's it, dig!

Emily I want to do well.

Fran Of course you do.

Woman Go on then!

Emily I can hardly manage as it is. All the work. And to look after a baby as well.

Fran It'd be really hard.

Emily I don't think I can do it.

Fran And then there's the money.

Emily I know. And Mum and Dad can't give me any more.

Fran You know I'd be willing to help . . .

Emily That's not fair! Oh, perhaps I should stop. Leave College. Give it all up.

Woman Look, it's falling down.

Emily But then. Later. I think I might blame it. Hate it. I've worked so hard.

Woman That's it, keep digging.

Emily If only there was more help. Somewhere at College for the baby to go. Someone to look after it while you were in lectures.

Fran Same where I work. Nowhere has anything like that.

Emily They don't want women to do both.

Boy Mum! Mum!

Emily But I want to keep it.

Woman Yes? Oh yes, it's lovely!

Emily I think I'll go mad trying to decide what to do.

Fran Em. You cry at night, don't you? I can hear you.

Emily I'm sorry. This must be awful for you.

Fran No. It's probably one of the biggest decisions you'll ever have to make. I just wish I could help you.

Emily These clothes I've got to buy for it. When you're at work, I walk for miles trying to find them. 'Cos I want the best things and I can't afford them. So I go from shop to shop, trying to get what I want. But cheap.

Fran   It's stupid, I don't know why you have to get all these things. Nighties, nappies, bibs.

Emily   I think it's so you've given something to the baby. Something from *you*. That's what they say anyway. Like, a start. Same as I have to give it a name too, even though they'll change it.

(She pauses.)

Emily   But all the women in the shops go gooey on me. 'When's it due?' they say. They all think I'm happy.

(She cries.)

Woman   Let's dig a moat now!

Fran   Oh Em!

Emily   I daren't even go to the classes. All the women there'll be the same. Fran, I'm frightened. What's it going to be like?

Fran   Don't worry. Look, I'll get some books. And we'll do the exercises together. In the front room. Throw the furniture away.

(They laugh.)

Emily   I'm missing Mum.

Fran   She's missing you.

Emily   I'm better here.

Boy   Is it finished now?

Woman   We'll just put a flag on it.

Fran   Em.

Emily   Mmmm?

Fran   You know that shawl? The one Mum gave you? Why don't you give that one to the baby. It's beautiful.

Emily   I've never worn it.

Fran   Yes, of course, you might want to save it.

Emily   No, it's a good idea. It's nicer than anything I've seen. And Mum gave it me. Like giving a bit of her too.

Fran   Yes.

Emily   Yes. Fran?

Fran   Mmmm?

Emily   Thank you.

SCENE 8   OCTOBER 1989

(*A café in Gloucester.*
Hannah *is with her boyfriend* **James**. *He's just bought tea.*)

Hannah   Thank you.

James   So what are you going to do?

Hannah   Hire a detective? Nothing I can do.

James   What do your parents say?

Hannah   I think they're a bit relieved. They'd said they'd help, but they were a bit upset. Especially Mum.

James   Scared you'd go off them.

Hannah   I know. I wouldn't. I do love them. Even Mum, though we row all the time.

James   Who doesn't?

Hannah   Dad says it's 'cos we're alike. Both bossy. Both always rushing about. Good with our hands.

James   Funny that. And you might be nothing like your real mum.

Hannah   I want to know. If I'm like Mum because I live with her, or if I'm like my real mum. I just want to know where I come from.

James   You might hate her.

Hannah That's what the man said. Or she might be dead. Or a tramp. I'll chance it.

James She might be a film star.

Hannah Yeah, Madonna. Don't be daft!

James You look nice today.

Hannah Why are mums the most important?

James Are they?

Hannah Just think. One day, three years' time. I'll just turn up on her doorstep.

James Will I know you then?

Hannah You don't lose people.

James Come on, let's go for a walk.

SCENE 9   NOVEMBER 1992

*(**Emily** and **Heather's** flat in London.*
***Emily** is now forty. She has just finished putting up some shelves.)*

Heather Come on, let's go for a walk.

Emily They look good, don't they?

Heather Best shelves I've ever seen.

Emily Don't mock. You know it's an achievement for me. Useless at anything like that.

Heather There's the phone. I'll go. Stop admiring them or they'll fall down.

Emily I'll get my coat.

*(**Heather** goes out. There is a pause, then **Heather** comes back into the room.)*

Heather It's for you!

Emily Who is it?

Heather Wouldn't say. A woman. Sounds a bit odd to me.

Emily   Someone wanting me to put shelves up for them probably.

(*She goes to the phone.*)

Emily   Hello?

(***Hannah*** *is at the other end of the phone.*)

Hannah   Is that Emily Summers?

Emily   Yes.

Hannah   Of 4, Beaumont Crescent?

Emily   Yes. Who is this?

Hannah   Is your middle name Alison?

Emily   Look, what is this?

Hannah   Please. I just want to make sure I'm right. Please answer my questions.

Emily   All right. Yes, that's my middle name.

Hannah   And did you live in Perranporth in Cornwall in 1973?

(*A long pause.*)

Emily   Yes.

Hannah   Does the date 15 December 1973 mean anything to you?

(*A very long pause.*)

Emily   Yes. Yes it does.

Hannah   My name is Hannah. I think the name *you* gave me was . . .

Emily   Eva.

SCENE 10   15 DECEMBER 1992

(*A split scene:*
First **Lionel** *and* **Edie's** *kitchen in Nottingham. They are sitting with their friend* **Marje***.*)

Edie   Eva.

Marje   That's nice. Another 'E', like you and Emily.

Lionel They called her Hannah, the people who adopted her.

Marje Ooh Edie, a granddaughter for you both. After all these years.

Edie It's her birthday today. Nineteen years old.

Lionel Four o'clock she's due at Emily's.

*(**Edie** looks at her watch.)*

Edie She'll be arriving any minute now, then.

*(**Jo** and **Michael's** kitchen. They live in Bristol now. **Jo** is fingering a jet brooch. **Michael** looks at his watch.)*

Michael She'll be arriving any minute now, then.

Jo Why did she have to choose her birthday to go?

Michael She's a romantic.

Jo I'm so afraid we'll lose her.

Michael You don't lose people.

*(**Emily** and **Heather's** kitchen in London. **Emily** is alone. There is a knock at the door. **Emily** goes to open it. **Hannah** is carrying a shawl wrapped in white tissue paper.)*

Emily Hello.

Hannah Hello.

(There is a pause.)

Emily Happy birthday.

(They smile.)

Talking Points

(For discussion in small groups, write each 'Talking Point' on a separate piece of card.)

1. What word is written on the brooch that Hannah gives Jo on her birthday? This is one of the birthday presents in the play. What's the other? What's so special about these particular presents?

2. Why is Jo nervous about Hannah meeting Emily?

3. Why is Hannah so determined to find her natural mother?

4. Why did Emily have her baby adopted?

5. How do you think Emily felt after the phone call from Hannah?

6. Do you think Emily and Hannah will become friends?

7. At what age was Hannah legally old enough to trace her natural parents? Do you think this is the 'right' age?

8. Should Edie and Lionel have the right to contact Hannah?

Investigations

1. Emily's baby is born in 1973. Though Emily knows she mustn't make contact with her daughter once she's been adopted, imagine that she decides to write her a letter that she hopes to be able to give her one day.

In the letter she tries to explain to her little girl the reasons why she is handing her over for adoption. It starts . . .

My dear little daughter . . .

How does it go on?

2. What three wishes might any parent wish for a new-born child?

Would the wishes be different for a girl and a boy? List the three wishes and say why you've chosen each one. Your list might be laid out something like this . . .

To my son/daughter
I wish . . . because . . .

3. If you decided to have a baby adopted, what one present would you give? Make a drawing of your gift and explain why you have chosen it.

4. *Either* (a) in pairs discuss together your ideas about: What happened at Hannah's first meeting with Emily? What did they do? What did they say? How did their meeting end?

Now, together with your partner, write the scene that takes place.

Or (b) Write a scene which shows what happens when Hannah leaves Emily's and goes to meet James – or another friend. Think about what kind of mood she is in. How much does she want to say about her meeting? What does James – or the friend – say to her? Does she intend to visit Emily again?

When you've written your scene, rehearse it and show it to the rest of the class. Do you all have very similar ideas of what took place at Hannah and Emily's or Hannah and James's meeting?

5. Some of the people in the story have agreed to take part in a daytime television show about adoption. They are going to talk to a studio audience about their experiences and answer any questions the audience may have.

Choose the characters in the play who would be the most suitable for interviewing. Who do you think would have most to say? Ask for volunteers to play each part.

Then select one or two people to present the show and chair the discussion. This isn't an easy job. It needs people who are good at organising, and at keeping order, and at summing things up when the debate is coming to an end. The rest of the class become the members of the audience. Split the class into those who think that children should be allowed to look for their natural parents . . . and those who don't.

Take time to prepare what you want to say, then organise your working space to make an appropriate setting for the show. Start by hearing the experiences of those involved in Emily and Hannah's story, then let the audience have their say.

6. Create a sound effects soundtrack for *The Birthday Present*. The action of the play moves around quite a bit: sound effects would be a good, simple way of suggesting all the different settings.

How would you create the effects for:

a Turkish bath
a village green in springtime
a café
a seashore?

Use whatever you can to conjure up the effects: old recordings, voices, musical instruments etc. And can anyone supply you with a Simon and Garfunkel record like the one that Emily and her friends listen to back in 1973 (p. 44)?

7. People give presents in this play. Try some imaginary present-giving in your group.

Sit in a circle, and choose someone to start the present-giving by miming handing over a parcel to the person on their left. The giver does not have a present in mind. As they pass on their gift they say: 'Because I like you I'm giving you this . . .'

The person receiving the present decides what they would most like to be given and finishes the sentence by saying what the present is and offering lots of thanks.

The present can be BIG . . . or small. It can be very expensive . . . or cost very little. It can be fantastical.

When everyone has had a chance to pass on and receive a present, work round the circle in the opposite direction. This time the present-giver decides what they want the present to be and tries to indicate through the way they mime the handover of the parcel (and possibly with sound effects) what the parcel contains. They still cannot name the present. It is up to the receiver to guess what is in the parcel. See how close they are to guessing it right. The game then continues round the circle.

BULLSEYE

Maria Oshodi

THE CHARACTERS

Paul Curtis, a black schoolboy
Neville Curtis, his dad
Glenda Curtis, his mum

Paul's schoolfriends:
Alex
Jackie
Matthew
Ross

'Coach': Paul's games teacher
Paul's form teacher
A doctor
A man in the old house
A nurse
A school helper

There are non-speaking parts for Paul's classmates and for members of the school football team.

About this play

Bullseye is about a disease called sickle cell anaemia. This is a blood condition which can affect young people from Africa and the Caribbean. It is a condition which is passed on from parents to children. It's an hereditary disease: that means it can't be 'caught' like a cold or measles.

Paul Curtis is ten when he finds out that he has sickle cell anaemia. For a while the disease doesn't seem to have much effect, so it's easy enough for Paul to pretend that there's not a lot wrong with him. Then he starts getting pains in his arms and legs. He can't play football like he used to: he can't run fast either or take part in any activity that will make him feel tired.

After a while, it becomes impossible for Paul to hide his illness . . . though that's what he'd like to do.

SCENE 1

*(A school medical room where a school helper is giving a girl some medicine in a glass. **Paul** comes into the room.)*

Paul   Miss?

Helper   Down in the medical room again, Paul? What is it this time?

Paul   I've got a pain.

Helper   Where?

Paul   My leg. It's like I've sprained it.

Helper   Well, I can only put a bandage on it. That's all I can do.

SCENE 2

*(**Paul's** bedroom: Paul's **mother** is scolding him.)*

Mum   Paul. Your bed's wet again! Ten years old and you're still doing it.

Paul   Mum, I'm sorry. Don't smack me.

Mum   Yes, I will smack you till you learn what the bed is for and what the toilet is for.

SCENE 3

*(The school playground: **Paul** is with a classmate, **Matthew**. **Matthew** pulls a face and points at **Paul's** leg.)*

Matthew   What's that?

Paul   A rash.

Matthew   You tramp! What kind of a rash?

Paul   I dunno.

Matthew It's called lergies.

Paul It's not! It's just a rash.

Matthew Don't come near me.

Paul It's all right. I'm going to the doctor about it on Friday.

Matthew Well, stay away from me until Friday then.

SCENE 4

*(The Doctor's surgery. **Paul** is there with his **mother**.)*

Mum Doctor, does Paul get these rashes because he's allergic to something?

Doctor Lots of children get rashes at his age. Just juvenile eczema. Nothing to worry about.

Mum But he's always tired . . . *and* he has headaches . . . He's been wetting his bed and now these swellings. What is it? What's wrong with him?

Doctor A mild case of gout. I'll prescribe you some pills. And we'll take a blood test just in case. You can come back if there's any more trouble . . . but there shouldn't be.

SCENE 5

*(The school sports field: **Paul** and **Ross** are with the games teacher, '**Coach**'.)*

Ross I don't want Paul on my side. He's useless.

Coach If you want to play football, Paul, you must try harder. Saying you're tired is no excuse. So, let's see you do the track twice with the others.

SCENE 6

*(Again in the Doctor's surgery: **Paul** is with his **mum and dad**.)*

Paul Hello, doctor.

Doctor   Sit down, all of you. ✗

*(They do. The **doctor** waits a while before he speaks.)*

Doctor   According to the blood test we took, it seems that Paul has got a rare blood group known as SS.

Mum   SS? ✗

Doctor   It means he has a disease called sickle cell anaemia.

Dad   What's that then? ✗

Doctor   It's a blood condition that affects people from Africa and the Caribbean. It attacks the red blood cells. It makes them curved like a sickle, instead of being round. It's handed down from parents to children.

Dad   You trying to tell me we gave Paul this thing?

Doctor   I'm afraid so.

Dad   There's nothing wrong with my blood.

Mum   Shut up and listen to the Doctor, Neville.

Doctor   Well, Mr Curtis, you might think there's nothing wrong with your blood because you don't suffer like your son, but both you and your wife seem to be carrying the AS sickle gene.

Dad   I don't see how I can be carrying a disease around with me and I don't even know about it. Who did I catch it from?

Doctor   It's an hereditary condition. You didn't catch it from anyone. You *can't* catch it. You're born with it, or born carrying it. And most people who carry it don't even know they've got it because they don't suffer any ill effects.

Mum   Will Paul get any worse? ✗

Doctor   Some of the time he'll be perfectly well; at other times he may be very ill. All I can advise is that he drinks six pints of water per day to keep his blood thin and flowing, and that you keep him warm so he doesn't get colds and infections. And make sure he doesn't tire himself out! I'll see you in three months' time to check his blood and give you some more pain killers.

Dad   Thank you, Doctor. ✘

Mum   Thank you. ✗

(They leave the surgery.)

Mum   Come on Paul, love. Did you hear what the doctor said? We've got to keep you warm, get you drinking lots of water . . . and we mustn't let you get tired.

Paul   Yeah, yeah! ✗

Mum   Come on then, repeat it.

Paul   Keep warm, drink a lot and don't get tired!

SCENE 7

*(One year later. **Paul** is at secondary school. He hasn't been suffering much from his disease. It seems to have been lying dormant. **Alex** and **Jackie** are waiting for **Paul** at the school gates.)*

Alex   Oi Jackie, where's Paul?

Jackie   There he is.

Alex   Paul, you coming training?

Paul   Yeah, give me a chance to catch up will you. Parker just got me in the hall as I was coming out. He was trying to sign me up for that archery thing.

*(**Alex** laughs.)*

Jackie   What's that then?

Alex   Didn't you hear it come over the tannoy at lunch-time?

Jackie   No. ✗

Paul   Yeah, they're starting archery after school.

Jackie   What, like Robin Hood?

Alex   Yeah, and they make you wear the green tights as well . . .

Paul   Parker was really trying to get me to go. He made it sound all right.

*(**Alex** puts on a really sarcastic voice.)*

Alex   Oh yeah! It's so interesting! It's on *World of Sport* on the telly every Saturday afternoon.

*(**Jackie** joins in the joke.)*

Jackie   Or if you don't want to see it on telly, you can go and see a live match at your local bow and arrow pitch.

Alex   I can't wait for my Dad to take me to the archery cup final at Wembley this year!

Jackie   Who would be mad enough to go to archery instead of football?

Alex   I bet Paul would.

Paul   No! No, I wouldn't. No way, Alex. I told Parker I was going to football instead.

Alex   And you'd better do better than you did last week . . .

Paul   What?

Jackie   Oh yeah. When he let the ball in the goal.

Paul   That wasn't my fault! How did I know Ross was going to slice the ball into our own goal.

Alex   That was so wicked!

Paul   Anyway . . . who's the fastest runner on the team? Me!

Alex   Me!

Paul   Me.

Alex   It's me!

Paul   I am.

Jackie   Any one's better than you, Paul. You run like a snail.

Alex   I'll race both of you.

Jackie   All right then.

Paul   Forget the race, just take it I'm the best.

Alex   No, we'll race for proof.

Jackie   All right, all right. From this lamp post . . . down to the end of the road.

Alex   No, that's too easy.

Paul   Let's do it tomorrow in the playground. I don't really feel like. . .

Alex   I know! What about over there. See that boarded up old house and the garden?

Jackie   Yeah?

Alex   You've got to run through the garden, touch the back wall and the first one back on the pavement is the winner.

Jackie   Right.

Alex   Yeah, Paul?

Paul   It looks a bit wild in there, and we might be trespassing.

Alex   Oh, come on!

Paul   All right then!

(They line up for the 'off'.)

Jackie   On your marks, get set, go! Come on Paul!

(They run into the garden of the house.)

SCENE 8

(In the garden: near the back wall. **Jackie** *and the boys scramble over rubbish, rubble and long grass.* **Paul** *is last. A man's voice calls out from the ramshackle house.)*

Man   Oi, you kids; get out of here!

*(**Alex** and **Jackie** stop. They're out of breath.)*

Alex   Who said that?

Jackie   Someone in the house.

*(A dog barks. The **man** calls again.)*

Man   If you don't clear out, I'm going to set my dog on you!

Jackie What are we going to do? How are we going to get back past the house?

Alex We'll have to get over the back wall. Come on Paul!

Jackie He's so slow, we're going to get caught.

(*Paul catches them up.*)

Paul There's someone coming . . .

Alex I know. The race is over. You lost anyway.

Paul That race doesn't count . . .

Alex Why not?

(*The dog barks again.*)

Jackie I'm climbing the wall before the dog bites me.

(*She starts getting up the wall.*)

Alex Quick, man!

Paul Wait for me! Jackie, I've got a pain in my leg; that's why I couldn't run.

Alex Your leg will be paining you badder when the dog bites it.

Jackie Come on Alex, help him. Here comes the man!

(*Alex and Jackie help Paul. He struggles to reach the top.*)

Man Clear off, the lot of you! If I catch you here again my dog will make such a meal of you, your own parents won't even recognise you!

Alex Jump!

Paul I can't. My leg. Don't pull me!

(*He cries out as the other two drag him off the wall.*)

SCENE 9

(*The other side of the wall. Alex and Jackie are running away. Paul is limping badly.*)

Alex Run!

Paul   I can't!

(Alex and Jackie stop. They wait for Paul.)

Alex   Stop mucking around, Paul.

Jackie   He's not.

Alex   What's wrong with him then? Sprained his leg?

Jackie   No.

Alex   Fractured it?

Jackie   No.

Alex   Broken?

Jackie   No.

Alex   What is it, then? Is he a cripple?

Paul   No I'm not!

Jackie   He's got . . .

Paul   Shut up Jackie!

Jackie   It's all right. You told *me* didn't you?

*(She speaks to **Alex**.)*

Jackie   He's got this disease called Sick cell or something.

*(**Alex** backs off and starts to run away. **Paul** calls after him.)*

Alex   A disease! Nasty!

Paul   Alex come back!

Alex   I don't want to get it.

Paul   You're black, Alex. You should know about sickle cell. You don't catch it.

*(He turns back to **Jackie**.)*

Paul   See what you've done. He's going to tell the whole class now. I should never have told you in the first place.

Jackie   I'll make sure he won't say anything.

Paul   You can't control Alex's mouth.

Jackie Yes I can. I promise.

Paul All right, then. Help me home now.

Jackie But I'm going to miss training!

Paul You owe me one after telling Alex.

Jackie OK, OK. Come on then; let's go.

(*Paul* hobbles off with the help of *Jackie*.)

SCENE 10

(*Paul's* home; a few days later. He is lying on the couch, half asleep.
His parents are sitting at the nearby dining-room table.
They are talking quietly, in the hope that **Paul** won't be able to hear
them.)

Mum . . . So he called me into his office, and asked me where I'd
been for three days. He hadn't got my message. He thought I
was just taking the time off for the sake of it. I had to tell him
about Paul.

Dad Well, when I told my boss that I had to stay at home because
my boy was sick and my wife had to go to work, he asked me
when was I going to be back.

Mum Well, you don't know do you?

Dad But Glenda, it's been four days now. Four days of him
drinking water, taking pain killers and having rest, and still the
boy's got pains in his legs. How much rest is he going to need
before it goes?

Mum We don't know. Not even the doctors know. We'll just have
to wait, and do the things the doctor told us to.

Dad Yes, yes; plenty of rest, water and pain killers, but for how
long! And, by the way, the school phoned. They want to know
what's going on.

Mum They want to know what's going on? Sickle cell anaemia is
what's going on! Did you tell them?

Dad Yes. They asked if we'd thought of sending him to a special
school. One that could cope with his handicap.

Mum   There's nothing wrong with his brain. He's normal. He's only got sickle cell.

Dad   They said they'd never heard of it, would you believe it? They were going to speak to the school doctor.

Mum   I hope they get a better explanation than we got.

Dad   Well, you can talk to him when he phones. They said he'd probably phone here.

Mum *(annoyed)*   And you said I would be here to take the call.

Dad   Well, I told my boss that I would be in tomorrow.

Mum   And I told mine that *I* would be!

Dad   There's nothing I can do. He's expecting me. We've got to get through an important menu.

Mum   Neville, I've been back for one day after three days away from work. What are they going to think of me if I have another day off.

Dad   Who cares? Tell them to stuff their job, and when Paul gets better you can get another one.

Mum   I like my job. I don't want to give it up.

Dad   It was your family that gave him this sickle cell, so you should . . .

Mum   What are you saying? I'm a strong healthy woman. Never a day's illness in my life. You're sicker than all of us, with your backaches and headaches.

Dad   Never!

Mum   Oh stop this, Neville. You know it's got nothing to do with it anyway. You heard what the doctor said. We both gave him the sickle cell and that's that!

*(**Paul** calls from the couch.)*

Paul   Mum, can I have a drink.

*(His **mum** goes to get him a drink. She whispers to Paul's **dad**.)*

Mum   We'd better keep our voices down!

SCENE 11

*(From **Paul's** couch: we hear his thoughts.)*

Paul It's a bit late to keep your voices down.

(He calls out.)

Paul Mum, can I have a Coke?

Mum You've got to drink six pints of water, Paul. Neville, how much water has Paul drunk today?

Dad I don't know. Give the boy a Coke if he wants one.

Mum You should have kept a check.

(She comes over to the couch with a glass.)

Mum I'm sorry Paul; you've got to drink some water. It's good for you.

*(**Paul** takes it and thinks . . .)*

Paul Good for me! If that means it's supposed to be good for the pain, then it isn't working.

Mum How's your pain?

*(**Paul** rolls over on his side.)*

Mum OK then. I'll leave you to get some sleep.

(She goes away and once again we hear what he's thinking.)

Paul Yeah, go away. I don't want you near me. There's nothing you can do. It feels like my legs are goal posts and Alex is kicking a pain ball against them, shot after shot. Those pain killers are no good. No good at tackling either. The sickle cell always gets the ball and keeps up the attack from when I go to sleep to when I wake up, day, after day, after day . . .

SCENE 12

*(**Paul's** bedroom; a few days later. He is feeling better. He talks to himself as he gets his bag ready for school.)*

Paul The sickle cell couldn't keep it up for ever! By day six it got tired, and the pain killers have moved in and are making a good defence. They've got the ball·and are keeping it well away. The sickle cell has gone back through the tunnel into the changing room to become a normal blood cell and I feel great. I'm ready for school, and training afterwards with Alex.

*(**Mum** calls to him.)*

Mum Come on Paul. It's ten past eight. You're going to be late.

Paul Mum, I can't find my football stuff.

Mum Forget about that today. You've only just got better. Let's just get you back to school and see how it goes.

Paul But I need it. I've got to train tonight for the game on Saturday.

*(**Mum** comes in carrying a box.)*

Mum Paul, your father and I were talking about you playing football, and we think that maybe you should give it a rest for a while.

Paul No Mum. Why? I feel all right. I haven't got pain or anything. Please give me my stuff. You've got it haven't you?

Mum It might be all this running around and tiring yourself out that's bringing on the sickle cell attacks, Paul. You've got to learn to do things that aren't going to make you ill again. Look, we were going to give you this later, but I'll show it to you now.

(She opens the box.)

Mum Your father went out especially and bought you it. Isn't it brilliant? It's an archery set.

Paul How did you know? Did you talk to the school? You did, didn't you?

(He knocks the box out of her hands as he dashes past.)

Paul I don't want it. No one's into archery. I want to play football just like the others.

(He runs out of the flat and slams the door.)

SCENE 13

*(At school: later that morning. Paul's **teacher** is talking to the class.)*

Teacher   We must remember to treat Paul kindly. Some things he can't manage, can you Paul? Would you like to tell the other children about it? No? All right then. I will . . . Paul has a disease called sickle cell anaemia which means his blood cells are a sort of banana shape, and they don't last for very long . . . and they don't go through his blood very easily like our round ones do. His cells all jam up in his veins sometimes, and the air that they carry stops getting around his body . . . so that causes him lots of pain. That's why he sometimes has to take his pills. Isn't that right, Paul?

*(There is an awkward silence in the classroom. **Paul** thinks . . .)*

Paul   I hate that stupid man. What's he showing me up for in front of the class. And I hate Mum and Dad for telling the school. Why couldn't they keep their big mouths shut?

SCENE 14

*(After school; in the corridor. **Paul** catches up with **Alex**.)*

Paul   Yo Alex!

Alex   All right Paul?

Paul   Where you going? Training?

Alex   Yeah.

Paul   Why didn't you wait for me?

Alex   Jackie said you probably wouldn't be able to go training any more.

Paul   Why?

Alex   Well, you know . . .

Paul   I'm not an invalid.

Alex   I never said you were, but . . .

Paul   Look, I'm all right. Do I look sick?

Alex Well no, not really.

Paul All right then, let's go! Have you got some spare trainers?

Alex Where are yours?

Paul I er, I forgot them.

Alex I haven't got any, but the coach might.

Paul Oh yeah, the coach. Listen Alex, when we get to training right, don't say anything to the coach about me.

Alex Why?

Paul Well there's no need really (*He pauses . . . then he lies.*) 'cos he . . . er . . . he already knows all about it. My Mum and Dad told him last week . . .

SCENE 15

(At the pitch and ten minutes into the game of football. 'Coach' yells from the side-lines.)

Coach Come on, come on! If I wanted slugs playing for me I would've dug some out of my garden. You're letting the cold weather slow you down. Wake up and get yourselves moving, or on Saturday, Crossfords are going to have that cup. Paul, move it! I've seen more life in the local graveyard. You were useless in goal last week; that's why you're in mid-field now and you're just as pathetic . . . Look, that's three times you've let the ball get away because you're about as fast as a sleeping cow. Put some power into those legs, and let's see some action before I die of boredom!

*(We hear **Paul's** thoughts . . .)*

Paul All right, then! Alex has got the ball now. I'm going to try and get in there. I'm catching up with him. We're running together. We're the same. All I have to do is tackle the ball now. But hold on, he's edging ahead of me. Come on legs, just a bit more push and I'll catch up with him again.

Coach Faster! Faster!

Paul I can't go any faster . . . and the gap is getting bigger.

Coach Come on Paul, move yourself!

Paul I'm trying. I want to, but my body doesn't. Oh God. I can't ignore the pain, biting like teeth into my arms and legs.

Coach Paul, don't let that ball get away!

Paul I've got to stop! I can't keep up any more!

(**Paul's** *legs give way under the pain and he collapses on the pitch. As he cries out, with the pain shooting up his legs and arms, everyone comes to a stand still. '**Coach**' runs over.*)

Coach What the hell's happened?

Paul Alex, Ross, please help!

(**Alex** *and* **Ross** *come forward. They kneel down next to* **Paul**.)

Alex What have we got to do? What did our teacher say?

Ross He's got some pills. Paul, where are your pills?

Coach Pills? What's wrong with him?

Alex I thought you knew. He's got this disease in his blood.

Ross Our teacher told us today.

Coach What?! Why in God's name didn't anyone tell me? How can he expect to play football in this state?

Ross What're we going to do?

Coach We'll have to get Gary on as a substitute.

Ross But what about Paul?

(**Paul** *cries out again.*)

Coach Where does it hurt?

Paul My arms. My legs.

Coach What part of your leg? The ankle?

Paul No.

Coach Your knee?

Paul No!

Coach   Your thigh then?

Paul   No, not one part, the whole thing!

Coach   Everyone stay where you are and don't go near him. I'm going to call the ambulance.

SCENE 16

*(A hospital ward: one week later. **Paul** is in bed. We hear what he's thinking.)*

Paul   Another one of those injections, that's what I want. They've put a drip into my arm, and sometimes they give me oxygen, but it's that injection that makes the pain go away . . . for a while. Only a little while though. Then all those cells begin to cram up again in my blood, and it's only the injection – like an arrow shooting into my arm – that goes straight to the target, the pain inside me. That's why I want another injection now!!

(He shouts out.)

Paul   Nurse!

*(A very busy, very tired **nurse** comes up to his bed.)*

Nurse   Yes Paul, what is it?

Paul   My pain's come back.

Nurse   There are other children in here, and they're just as much in pain as you Paul. You don't hear them screaming and shouting. Please have some consideration.

Paul   But I can't help it.

Nurse   Well, there's nothing I can do. You're just going to have to wait until it's time for your next injection.

Paul   I can't wait another three hours!

Nurse   We can't give you any more yet.

Paul   What am I going to do then?

Nurse   You'll just have to bear it, lovey. Look! Here's your dad come to see you. That will cheer you up.

*(Paul's **dad** comes over to the bed.)*

Dad Hello Nurse! How is everything?

Nurse As well as can be expected. Paul seems to be in a little bit of pain, but his next injection isn't due yet, so I'll be back to give him that in an hour or so.

*(She leaves and Paul's **dad** sits at the bedside.)*

Dad Hello Paul. I brought you some comics and chocolates . . . oh, and before I forget, Jackie and Alex rang up to say they were coming in to see you later. How you feeling? The pain still bad?

Paul Yeah. When can I go home, Dad?

Dad You're still in pain, Paul. You can't go home until that's gone. It was a bad, bad crisis you had this time, and it's only the hospital that can help you get better. This sickle cell is a serious thing. Me and your mother tried to make you understand.

Paul Where is Mum?

Dad She's not feeling so good. Too much worry, you know. The doctor came and told her to rest in bed for a couple of days.

Paul I suppose if I'd listened to her and not gone to football, I might not be here now and I might not have caused so much trouble.

Dad Well, that might be true. You see Paul, you've got to start helping yourself. You can't do things that you know will make you bad.

Paul You mean . . . stop playing football.

Dad You could always take up something else in its place.

Paul Like archery!

Dad Well . . . if it's going to keep you out of hospital.

Paul But it's going to be stupid. They make you wear green tights.

74 **Dad** What?

Paul That's what Alex said.

Dad Take no notice of what Alex said. I can promise you that they do not make you wear green tights.

Paul But nobody does archery, Dad.

Dad You've just got to accept that you can't be like the others and do what they do. Listen Paul, let me ask you a question . . . What do I do for a job?

Paul You're a cook.

Dad Otherwise known as a chef. Yes, that's right. And do you know how I became a chef?

Paul No.

Dad Because back home, I couldn't get into the police force. All my friends were leaving home and going to join the army or the police. I didn't want to join the army, but I wanted to join the police. They wouldn't have me though, because I was too short. There was absolutely nothing I could do about it. Then my grandfather became ill, and I stayed at home to look after him, and cook for him. Even though he was ill, he loved his food and I began to love the cooking I did for him, so I decided to do it professionally. When I told all my friends who were in the army and the police, they just laughed . . . but that didn't stop me. And now . . . am I a good chef? Remember that dinner we had on Christmas day!

Paul You're a good chef.

Dad I'm a better chef than most of my friends are policemen or soldiers! You never know Paul; if you took up archery, then you might become a better shot than your friends are football players, and you might be winning cups and medals when they're still . . .

Paul Cups and medals! Could I win those?

Dad If you got good enough and entered tournaments.

Paul Wicked!

*(**Alex** and **Jackie** come into the ward.)*

Jackie Hello, Paul.

Alex All right Paul? We had a really brilliant game this afternoon. Won Crossfords three nil.

Jackie Crossfords are rubbish!

Alex We are the champions!

Dad Shh!

Alex Paul, is there a telly in this place?

Paul Yeah. In the visitors' room.

Jackie Great, just in time to watch the big match.

Paul Well I was looking in the newspaper this morning and there's this Robin Hood film on the other side. I think I want to see that.

(**Alex** and **Jackie** look at each other in amazement.)

Alex
Jackie } What?

(**Paul** looks at his **Dad** and smiles. His **dad** smiles too.)

Dad Bullseye!

Talking Points

(For discussion in small groups, write each 'Talking Point' on a separate piece of card.)

1. Why doesn't Paul want his classmates to know about his illness?

   What is he afraid of?

   Is he ashamed of being ill?

2. Why does Alex run away when he finds out that Paul has sickle cell anaemia?

3. Who do you think should stay off work to look after Paul; his mum or his dad?

4. Why does Paul's father suggest that Paul takes up a new sport?

   Why does Paul agree?

Investigations

1. Paul decides to take up archery.

Write a magazine article which tells how successful he becomes in his new sport. The article should be really inspiring. It should show how one young boy learnt to conquer his illness and become a successful athlete – against all odds!

Think of a suitable title for your article.

Attach a note to the article, telling the magazine's picture department what kind of photographs should go with the story.

2. Imagine that the magazine story gets taken up by a television series. Every week this series shows a programme about somebody who has been very brave and who has managed to overcome some kind of illness or disability. The programme is designed to show that illness need not be a handicap.

This week's episode is all about Paul!

In groups, prepare and show an excerpt from the programme. Decide on the main points you want to make and choose the characters who'll feature in this televised version of Paul's story. For example, the programme presenter, interviewers, Paul himself, his parents, his mates, his teachers, his archery coach . . . etc.

Work out what you'll show and then present your excerpt to the others.

3. Paul doesn't want to tell his class about his illness. His teacher does it for him. Do you think he was right to do so?

In pairs, act out the conversation that takes place before the lesson on p. 70.

First, Paul tells the teacher about his illness. Then the teacher tries to persuade Paul that he ought to let the rest of the class know . . . so that they can be more understanding.

How will *your* conversation end up? Will Paul agree to tell his classmates? Will the teacher decide to do it for him?

Let the others listen to what was said in your conversation. Have they got any comments or suggestions to make about the way the teacher tries to persuade Paul?

4. Paul may not want his friends to know that he's ill because he's scared that they won't have anything to do with him any more. He might become a sort of outcast . . . someone who is always on the outside.

In groups of five or six, make a tight circle with everyone linking arms and facing inwards – all except for one person who *agrees* to stand outside the circle and be 'the outsider'.

It's their job to try and get into the circle, either by talking their way in or by pushing their way in. The others stay silent and work together to keep them out. Give yourself a time limit! If the outsider doesn't manage to get into the circle in the time allowed, swap over and ask for another *volunteer*.

What does it feel like to be on the outside? Is it fun to begin with? Does it get more and more frustrating as time goes on?

5. Paul's mum and dad seem to have their own problems coping with Paul's illness. Things get so bad that Paul's mother becomes ill herself.

Imagine that you are able to talk to them before matters get to this stage, and see what advice and help you could give them.

Choose two people to play the mum and dad. The rest of you act as a group of health workers (or counsellors) at the local hospital. You may not be able to give them much medical advice, but you can certainly listen to their problems, and maybe suggest ways in which they could help each other.

Someone will need to take charge of the meeting, but it's up to Paul's parents to tell the group what they would like to talk about. At the end of the meeting each of the health workers (or counsellors) can write up a report, giving a summary of what was said and adding a list of suggestions to make things easier for Paul's parents.

6. Alex runs away from Paul when he finds out that Paul is suffering from a disease. He doesn't stop to think or to ask questions – he just runs! He's like a lot of people who get frightened – or sickened – by the thought that someone is suffering from a disease. Often, they don't really know much about it. Their fears may be caused by ignorance.

Help to put the facts straight!

Bullseye tells us that sickle cell anaemia is an inherited blood condition. It's passed on from a parent to a child. It can't be caught like a cold or the 'flu.

Design a poster that will help to make the public more aware of this fact . . . and put a stop to the kind of reaction that we saw from Alex. Make the design as eye-catching as possible and keep your message short and snappy! You need to grab people's attention.

7. Another way of getting Paul's story across to young people is to make it into a serious comic strip.

Choose an incident – or a series of incidents – that you'd like to work on. It could be . . . when Paul finds out that he's got the disease, or when he tries to climb out of the garden with Alex and Jackie, or when he collapses on the football pitch.

Make two or three drawings for one episode of the comic strip. Put a headline or caption at the top of each drawing, and give the characters speech bubbles.

If you decide to present *Bullseye* on stage, here are some practical hints to help with the performance.

1. Scenes 1–5 are very short. They are almost like a series of 'snap-shots'. The action should cut very quickly from one scene to the next. So, set up the different locations or 'rooms' in different parts of the acting area with the other characters 'frozen' in their places until Paul walks into the 'snap-shot' and brings it to life. At the end of each scene he moves on quickly to the next.

2. As the play develops, Paul begins to share his thoughts with the audience. At these moments, you could 'freeze' the action around him, or fade the lighting on the rest of the characters and leave Paul in the spotlight. During the football match in Scene 15, you could try acting out the game in slow motion, and tape Paul's thoughts to play over the scene as a kind of commentary.

In this scene, you could cast two people to play Paul. When Paul begins to talk to the audience, one person would perform Paul's actions, while the other one voiced his thoughts.

THE LAST CUCKOO

John Wood

THE CHARACTERS

Alex, a London boy, on holiday in Somerset with his aunt and uncle

Uncle Don

Aunt Barbara

Andrew ⎫
Allison ⎭ twins who make friends with Alex on holiday

Ella ⎫
Frank ⎭ from an old people's home

Marjory, Frank's daughter

Sonia, Alex's mum

There is a non-speaking part for Alex's dad.

About this play

Alex is twelve. He is sent away for the summer to stay with his uncle and aunt in Taunton, Somerset. His mum and dad are having problems with their marriage, and want time on their own to sort things out. When Alex arrives at his uncle and aunt's house he is feeling miserable and angry. He is very difficult to deal with.

His uncle Don works in an old people's home. He takes Alex with him one day. Alex hates it there. He thinks the old people are stupid and disgusting, especially Ella and Frank who seem to be in love and who are planning to get married.

With the help of two new friends, Andrew and Allison, Alex plays a trick on the old couple. But the trick backfires, and Alex finds out that the old people aren't stupid and disgusting at all, and that they have a lot to teach him.

There are just three young people in this play: the three As – Alex, Andrew and Allison. All the other characters are adults. Two of them are old people, so there are quite a few acting challenges here. If you're playing one of the old people, try to avoid using 'funny', croaky voices and giving a comic performance. See if you can get away from this kind of acting, and play the part sensitively, so that your audience gets a true picture of the real feelings behind the words.

SCENE 1

*(In the train: **Alex** and his mother **Sonia** are on the final leg of their journey from London to Taunton in Somerset. **Sonia** is reading, and every so often she stares up at **Alex**. **Alex** stares back until she continues reading. She suddenly looks up and speaks.)*

Sonia   Don't blame me. There's no point in you sitting there blaming me. Your dad and I need the break, Alex. We want to find out if we can still live together. That's important isn't it?

Alex   How long before we get there?

Sonia   About 25 minutes. We're due in Taunton at 3.18. Try and drop this now Alex, and enjoy yourself. You've always got on with your uncle Don . . . and there's nothing wrong with your aunty Barbara. You're not helping the situation with all these moods. Coping with your father not speaking is bad enough without you starting!

Alex   Thought you said the train was late.

Sonia   You don't want to understand do you? Well, carry on. Thank God I'm going to get a rest.

*(**Alex** looks out of the window.)*

Sonia   Your father should have brought you down here. He could do with a bit of reality. He lives in cloud cuckoo land half the time. You take after him . . .

SCENE 2

*(At the station **Alex** and **Sonia** are met by **Don** and **Barbara**. **Sonia** is taking the next train back, so they say goodbye to her there. **Alex**, **Don** and **Barbara** arrive at No. 13 Cross Street.)*

Don   Go ahead and open the door for us Alex, there's a good lad.

*(He gives him the keys and **Alex** walks up the garden path. **Don** turns to **Barbara**.)*

Don   Those geraniums need a drink.

Barbara   Not as much as I do.

(**Don** *calls to* **Alex**.)

Don   Haven't you got that door open yet?

Alex   Yeh.

Don   In you go then and have a look round. Mind the cat. (*To* **Barbara**.) He's going to be hard work.

Barbara   So was Tiger when you brought her home. She only needed a bit of love.

Don   Just like me.

Barbara   Get away. We ought to change her name now you know – Sheba.

Don   No way.

(**Alex** *appears at the door.*)

Alex   Your cat just bit me for nothing. I hate it here.

Barbara   Here we go. (*To* **Alex**.) Let's have a look at that wound.

Alex   No.

(*He turns and goes into the house.*)

Barbara   Tiger number two.

Don   All he needs is a bit of love.

SCENE 3

(*The next day.* **Barbara** *has left for her work as a secretary.* **Don** *works across the road as a gardener in 'The Grange' – an old people's home. He and* **Alex** *are walking along a driveway bordered by a high hedge.*)

Alex   I don't want to help with any jobs.

Don   All right. You needn't. It's a nice place to play.

Alex   I don't play.

Don   Well there's plenty of nice people to meet.

(**Alex** *pulls a face.*)

Don   What *do* you want to do?

Alex   Nothing.

Don   Oh, I've always wanted to do that too.

Alex   I hate it here!

Don   You'll get used to it.

Alex   Its boring. There's loads to do in London. There's nothing here.

Don   I thought that's what you wanted to do. Nothing!

(**Alex** *pulls another face.* **Don** *smiles.*)

Don   This is where I work.

(*They walk through a gate and pass lawns, flowerbeds and a shrubbery. A group of old people sit in chairs on a terrace.*)

Alex   Nobody wants them do they?

Don   What makes you think that?

Alex   Wouldn't be in a home then, would they?

Don   They're all loved by someone Alex.

(**Alex** *stops and points.*)

Alex   Look at them two. Kissing! Urrgh.

Don   What's wrong with that?

Alex   They're old aren't they?

Don   So?

Alex   Old people don't go round doing that. You don't see them doing that in London.

Don   Come and say 'hello'.

Alex   No way.

(***Don*** *calls out to a couple on the seat.*)

Don   Morning Ella, Frank. Nice morning for a cuddle.

Ella   Come on over if you want one.

Don   I'm too busy.

Ella   So am I. See you later, Don.

Don   They've been courting some time. Wedding bells soon, I expect.

Alex   They can't get married. They can't have kids. It's stupid.

Don   I think they want to tell the world they love one another.

Alex   They're loopy.

Don   That's why your mum and dad got married.

Alex   What's the point in getting married when you're going to die? They're really old.

Don   Wouldn't you like your mum and dad to still be in love when they're that age?

Alex   No.

Don   Sometimes Alex, you're really stupid.

(***Don*** *walks towards an arch in a high wall.*)

Don   Come on!

Alex   No.

Don   What are you doing now?

Alex   I'm going to look round on my own.

Don   That's OK but don't go outside the grounds, and be back up here by eleven. Got your watch on? You'll hear a gong anyway, that's when we go and have coffee.

(***Alex*** *walks off down a path that runs alongside the high wall. Suddenly he hears voices and he moves into the cover of the bushes and watches.* ***Allison*** *and* ***Andrew Doran*** *appear on top of the wall.*)

Allison   See. There aren't any apples.

Andrew   I didn't say there were.

Allison   Well, there aren't! What is this place? A hospital. I bet it's a hospital.

Andrew   No. It's where they burn people when they're dead, isn't it? They're all like this . . . lawns and flowers.

Allison   I bet it's full of ghosts.

Andrew   Yeh. The garden of the living dead. Ghouls.

Allison   Spook Hall.

Andrew   Death House. I bet they all come out at night sliming over the lawns looking for flesh.

Allison   Your breath stinks!

Andrew   No!

Allison   You been eating garlic?

Andrew   Keeps you safe from werewolves.

Allison   You believe anything you read don't you?

Andrew   No! I read your diary and I didn't believe that.

Allison   You keep out of my diary.

Andrew   I'm not in it. I'm not 'Jason with deep blue eyes'.

Allison   You little creep.

(She starts to push him off the wall.)

Andrew   Get off.

*(**Alex** steps out from his hiding place. They stop fighting and stare at him.)*

Alex   Do you want to see some nearly dead people? There's loads in here.

*(**Allison** and **Andrew** jump down from the wall.)*

Alex   Come on, I'll show you, but you have to keep quiet.

*(He leads them through the bushes to a large yew tree behind where **Ella** and **Frank** sit holding hands. He points and they take turns to peep. **Alex** whispers.)*

Alex   Nearly dead.

*(The other two nod and smile. Suddenly **Ella** speaks very loudly.)*

Ella   What do you think, our Frank? All or nothing?

*(**Alex** mimes 'deaf' and points to his ears. The other two agree.)*

Frank   You've got a loud voice on you, Ella Cooper.

Ella   Me? You should have heard my mother. She died shouting. Penny for your thoughts, Frank? Come on now . . . what's bothering you?

*(**Frank** is silent.)*

Ella   How old are you – seventy-three?

*(**Alex** mimes having a heart attack.)*

Frank   I'm not like you, however old I am.

Ella   Don't go all peaky on me. Do you love me? Come on . . . kiss and make-up.

*(**Alex** mimes being sick.)*

Ella   Look at you, po-face. You'll never get a lass if you carry on like this you know.

Frank   I was married forty-four years.

*(**Alex** signals he must be mad.)*

Ella   Aye and pity her if she had half the trouble I get.

Frank   Don't talk like that.

Ella   Just my big mouth. Don't take no notice. Now come on: out with it! What's troubling you that I can't get two words out of you?

Frank   My Marjorie is coming down from Birmingham next week. Got a letter this morning.

Ella   What does she say, your dutiful daughter?

Frank   She wants to have a talk with me.

Ella   I knew this was coming. You've got to stand up to her Frank. It's your life.

Frank   I know . . . I'd better go. I said I'd give Don a hand in the greenhouse this morning.

Ella   Go on. Off you go. I've had more than three sentences out of you – I should be so lucky. Pick me a nice ripe tomato for my lunch.

Frank   See you in the dining-room.

Ella   Don't look so worried, Frank. It might never happen.

(He goes off towards the kitchen garden.
Alex whispers to the others.)

Alex   See how he walks. He'll be dead before he gets there.

(Ella has heard something. She calls out.)

Ella   Who's that?

(Alex motions for them to be quiet. He tries a bird whistle.)

Ella   A bird.

(The others are highly amused. Alex cups his hands and produces a pigeon sound.)

Ella   A pigeon.

(The three are falling about in silent laughter. Alex produces his masterpiece – a cuckoo call.)

Ella   It's a long while since I heard a cuckoo. What was it Gran used to say? 'Tell a cuckoo a secret and you'll always meet it, whenever you "cuckoo".'

(Alex nearly falls over, with trying to hold in his laughter.)

Ella   Let's try. It needs to be something I've never told anyone before.

(She thinks, and then she calls out.)

Ella   Cuckoo, I'm scared. That's why I talk so loud. I'm scared nobody likes me? Did you hear that?

(Alex is laughing so much he can't make another cuckoo call, so Ella moves off towards the house then shouts back.)

Ella   Now you know my secret we must meet whenever I call.

*(This time **Alex** responds with a 'cuckoo'. She turns and goes. **Alex**, **Allison** and **Andrew** explode with laughter.)*

Andrew It's a mental home! They're all mental!

Alex Good, eh?

Allison How do you do that with your hands?

Alex Easy.

(He cups his hands and does a cuckoo call.)

Andrew She really thought it was a cuckoo. Did you hear her? 'That's why I talk so loud.' Mental.

Alex What about him? She was trying to get him to kiss her. Sicko!

Andrew Kiss of death!

Alex Yeh. Nearly dead giving the kiss of death.

Allison You two are sick.

Andrew We could have killed them.

Alex No need. They'll be dead by tomorrow.

Andrew Do you know why there's tall trees in graveyards, 'cos of all the dead bodies. They make them grow.

*(**Allison** has been practising and blows a pigeon call.)*

Allison Done it!

Alex You'll never do the cuckoo, though. Do you want a wine gum?

Andrew Ta.

Allison Ta.

Alex Are you two twins?

(They nod.)

Allison Do you live here?

Alex My uncle works here. I'm staying with him. My parents have gone abroad for a holiday.

Allison   Where?

Alex   Dunnow.

(The twins smile at one another.)

Alex   They have!

Allison   Didn't say they hadn't.

Andrew   There's a blackbird up there.

(They all look up.)

Andrew   You got an air gun?

*(**Alex** shakes his head. Then he says . . .)*

Alex   She really thought it was a cuckoo.

(The twins don't respond this time.)

Alex   We could build a tree house if you like. Up there.

Allison   We haven't got any planks.

Andrew   Or a saw.

Alex   I can get some. Don't go away.

Allison   What's your name?

Alex   Alex.

Allison   The three As. Andrew, Alex and Allison.

Alex   That can be the name of the gang if you want.

(He turns and runs off.)

Andrew   That can be the name of the gang if you want. He's mental.

Allison   So are you. Listen.

(She blows a perfect cuckoo call.)

Allison   He reckons he's so clever.

*(**Andrew** smiles and drops a stone on a black beetle.)*

SCENE 4

(Alex is racing up towards the greenhouses. He meets Don coming down the path.)

Don   Had a good time?

Alex   No.

Don   Only six weeks to go.

(They walk down the path together.)

Alex   I want some planks and a hammer and some nails. Well? Can I have 'em?

Don   Yes, if you knew how to ask for them. Alex, you might be mad at the world and especially your mum and dad 'cos they're having a rough time, but don't take it out on the rest of us. Please. What do you want them for?

(Alex walks on in silence.)

Don   Look I'll make a deal. You take what you want from the potting shed up there –

(He has no time to finish as Alex runs back up the path. He reaches the yew tree where Alex and Allison are waiting.)

Alex   Come on, I've got everything we need. Come on.

Allison   What are we going to do in this tree house?

Alex   Spy on people. Come on.

(He runs ahead.)

Allison   Do you want to spy on people?

Andrew   Don't mind, long as we don't get caught.

(They move off after Alex.)

SCENE 5

(In Don and Barbara's house nearly one week later.)

Barbara   Where does he get to every day? Is he all right?

Don Don't ask me. He'll hardly speak. Has he spoken to you at all?

(She shakes her head.)

Don If he goes on bottling everything in like this he'll explode.

Barbara And blow us all to pieces. I'll have another try this weekend. The Barbara Norris box of tricks.

Don Don't try bribes. I did that – he just took the wood and ran off.

Barbara Serves you right. Where is he now?

Don I said he could go over the home for an hour this evening.

Barbara What does he do over there?

Don He's been building something. It must be a den. It was raining all day yesterday and I still didn't see him.

Barbara That fits. He's started asking for sandwiches. A den. Poor little lad.

Don I've told him to keep well clear of matron. I can just imagine what she would think about little boys playing at dens.

Barbara Poor Miss Taylor.

Don It's poor everybody tonight as far as you're concerned isn't it?

Barbara A little understanding is all people need.

Don What about me?

Barbara Get your own supper.

Don I thought as much.

SCENE 6

*(**Alex, Andrew** and **Allison** are in the tree house overlooking the seat.)*

Alex Here she comes, the mad woman. Your turn to cuckoo, Allison.

Allison You can do it.

Alex   You do it really well, go on.

Allison   No.

Alex   Do you want to have a try, Andrew?

Andrew   No thanks.

Alex   Here she comes. Watch this.

(*The twins look at one another.* **Alex** *cuckoos.* **Ella** *comes over.*)

Ella   Are you there, cuckoo?

(**Alex** *answers with his cuckoo call and looks to the others to join in the fun but they don't.*)

Ella   Listen, she's coming tomorrow. His daughter. She doesn't like me and she doesn't want him marrying me. I want you to keep an eye on him and don't let him weaken. He's not a strong man. If only you could talk. I'd love to know what she says to him. I'll tell him to bring her over here – private like – so you can hear it all. If everything else fails, fly out and do your business on her hair. I must be going. Daft isn't it talking to a cuckoo.

(*She gets up and leaves.*)

Alex   Batty old cow.

Allison   I think she's sad.

Alex   She's going to bring him over so we can hear everything. That's brilliant. She wants us to spy on them, but she doesn't realise we're already spying on her.

Allison   Let's find a new game, shall we?

Andrew   Yeh.

Alex   No!

Andrew   I'm fed up sitting up here all the time.

Allison   Not much fun is it?

Alex   You get sandwiches every day.

Andrew   Cheese.

Alex So? What's up with you two? She's going to bring him and his daughter over here tomorrow. We'll hear the lot.

Allison Let's have a vote.

Alex About what?

Allison What to do tomorrow?

Alex We're coming here!

Andrew We're getting bored of coming up here every day, even when it rains.

Allison And having you tell us what to think.

Alex What else are you going to do? This was my idea. It's great. Nobody knows we're up here.

Allison So what.

Alex Well, that's what's good about it. She's fooled. She believes it. Don't you get it?

Allison You're not very nice, are you?

Alex Me?

Andrew Don't you feel sorry for her?

*(**Alex** turns on **Andrew**.)*

Alex All *you* do is kill things.

Andrew It's better than this.

Alex Don't bother coming then. Either of you. It's my idea. It doesn't need you two eating my sandwiches.

Allison You're sick!

Alex *You* will be if you try coming up here tomorrow. And don't do anything to my tree house if you know what's good for you.

(He climbs down and leaves.)

Andrew What's up with him?

Allison He has to get his own way all the time.

Andrew What are we doing tomorrow?

Allison   Teaching him a lesson.

(*The twins smile at one another.*)

SCENE 7

(*Later, when **Alex** is in bed, there is a knock on his door.*)

Alex   Yeh?

Barbara   Your mum's on the phone, Alex. She'd like a word with you.

Alex   I'm tired.

Barbara   She'd like to speak to you a lot. So would your dad . . . They're worried about you. I've said you're all right –

Alex   I don't need to talk to them then.

Barbara   Shall I tell them anything for you? Send them your love.

Alex   No!

(*He turns over and buries his head in his pillow. She returns downstairs and picks up the phone.*)

Barbara   Hello Sonia. I'm sorry love, he still won't speak to you. (*She listens.*) No, no, don't do that. Give him another few days. Maybe something'll bring him round. All right love. No, not at all. Don't you worry.

(*She puts the phone down and speaks to **Don**.*)

Barbara   She's worried sick. What are we going to do? We can't force him to talk to them. She said she'll come down and fetch him back.

Don   He's taken hold of himself so tight he thinks the world will fall apart if he lets go.

Barbara   Maybe it will. He's making me angry and sad both at the same time. He was always such a happy lad.

Don   He's in secondary school now. He might be getting bullied. Might be the teachers.

Barbara Well, it's not our problem. There's only so much help you can give some people and then it's up to them.

Don What happened to 'poor little lad'.

Barbara I don't think he's very nice.

Don Well, you can't cure that with kind words.

Barbara It's a pity, when you think what he used to be like.

Don Puppies grow into dogs that bite, that's the way of the world.

Barbara I wish it wasn't.

SCENE 8

*(The next day **Alex** is in his tree nest bright and early waiting for **Frank** and watching the clouds build up in the sky. Everyone seems to be avoiding the tree seat today. He eats his sandwiches for lunch and waits. With rain threatening, he sees **Frank** and his daughter approaching. They sit down.)*

Marjory Are you all right Father? You seem fidgety.

Frank It's tomorrow.

Marjory What is?

Frank Tomorrow's the fifteenth.

Marjory Yes.

Frank August.

Marjory You're not making any sense.

Frank Your mother died five years since. Tomorrow.

Marjory It's good that you remember.

Frank Someone has to. She was all the world to me . . .

Marjory Then I don't understand what all this talk is about you getting married –

Frank No! You wouldn't understand. You live your life without loving anyone. You love *things*. Well, I love people and I need loving. So I've found someone who loves me – Ella – and I love her.

Marjory   Listen, Mike and I have discussed it and we can't take on any more responsibilities.

Frank   What do you mean?

Marjory   You've just not thought this through have you? If you remarry it means that Mike and I have a stepmother. If anything happens to you, we would be responsible for her. Now it costs a lot of money to keep you in here. We can't afford another responsibility —

Frank   Stop it. Stop it. You want to tell me you can't afford me.

Marjory   No.

Frank   Never in my life. Never did I count a single penny for you.

Marjory   I'm not talking about that —

Frank   No. No. No. I love Ella. If you can't afford that, then get out, get out.

Marjory   You're obviously having one of your turns. I'm going to get the matron.

*(She leaves. The **twins** appear from the bushes and walk up to **Frank**.)*

Allison   There's a boy in that tree whose been spying on you.

Frank   No! Never! Nothing! Gone! Love. Lo— Lo— Lo— Lo—

*(His speech deteriorates into unintelligible sounds and his head falls to one side. **Alex** has climbed down from the tree.)*

Andrew   What's up with him?

Alex   Don't you know?

Andrew   You've killed him. That's what you've done. He's dying. You can stand and watch him; that's what you like isn't it?

*(The **twins** run. **Alex** speaks to **Frank**.)*

Alex   I'm sorry, I wasn't really spying, someone asked me to.

*(Then **Alex** sees the **Matron** coming and runs.)*

SCENE 9

*(Next morning at **Don** and **Barbara's**. **Alex** is still not up.)*

Don   He's late this morning. I wonder if Frank made it through the night?

Barbara   Poor Frank. What brought it on?

Don   Who knows? His wife's anniversary, seeing his daughter, getting married . . . I suppose at some point his brain said 'Too much mate' and poof!

Barbara   All things he could control. It's what you can't control does that.

Don   What was it then?

Barbara   He was strong. He was fit. He used to help you.

Don   Something brought it on.

Barbara   I don't suppose we'll ever know now, but I've got my suspicions.

*(**Alex** enters.)*

Barbara   We were talking about Frank over the road.

Don   You know the two who sit on the seat together. He's had a stroke.

Alex   Is he dead?

Barbara   No. *(Then, in a matter of fact way.)* Do you want cornflakes?

Alex   How can you talk like that?

(He slams out of the door.)

Barbara   What on earth is wrong with him?

Don   You were a bit callous –

Barbara   Oh, so now he's the sensitive one is he? He doesn't seem to care who he walks on.

Don   There's no need to fly off the handle.

Barbara I've put up with his moods for a week now and suddenly I'm the one that's got size ten boots. Well, it's not on. Get him back in here.

Don Barbara.

Barbara No. I've had enough.

Don Darling, he was right. He was right.

Barbara Why is he right?

Don Because for some reason best known to himself he was being sensitive and we weren't. Maybe he's changing. Maybe he'll change some more – if you say sorry.

Barbara Oh. no.

Don We're the grown-ups.

Barbara He owes me twenty million apologies.

Don Luckily you owe him only one so it won't take long to say.

Barbara All right, you win.

Don Not a question of winning. Question of what's right.

SCENE 10

*(Later that day **Don** sees **Ella** walking towards the yew tree. He goes over and puts an arm round her.)*

Don You don't mind, do you? How is Frank?

Ella Fighting. The stroke's affected his speech. He can't say anything. That bit of him's gone.

Don He'll win through and so will you. You've got the cure Ella – love. Just make sure he gets plenty, and we'll make sure *you* do.

Ella Thanks Don. He used to love helping you in that greenhouse.

Don And he will again. Barbara sends her love. We're all thinking of you both.

*(In the tree house **Alex** has heard all this. **Don** leaves and **Ella** sits on the seat.)*

Ella Well, little cuckoo. See how my voice has gone small. That's 'cos I'm not worried about me today. Just him. He's had a stroke after he talked to her. Part of his brain stopped working – just a little bit – he can't speak any more. Sits there staring at me. But he can't say anything. He wants to, I know. I can see it in his eyes. I want to know what it is he's trying to tell me. What is it? There's something he wants to say. I know.

*(She sits crying gently. **Alex** climbs down the tree and goes to her. She holds his hand. After a while he says quietly and with dignity . . .)*

Alex He said he loved you.

Ella Bless you. Bless you. Thank you.

SCENE 11

*(A month later at the end of the holiday a car arrives outside No. 13. **Sonia** and **David**, Alex's parents get out. **Alex** comes down the garden to greet them.)*

Alex Hi Mum, hi Dad. You'll never guess what happened today. Frank said 'yes'. You see he can't speak, so Ella and me worked out this system where he does one squeeze for 'no' and two for 'yes'. And they're going to get married. Great, isn't it? What's been happening in smoke city?

Sonia Your dad and I have done some talking.

Alex Good.

Sonia And we've decided that we need you there. We thought we could work it out between us, but we realised there were three of us not two.

Alex Great. You don't say much do you Dad? No, don't spoil it now. Come and meet Frank, he can't stop talking since he lost his voice. Come on!

SCENE 12

(In the lounge at 'The Grange' – the old people's home.)

Alex Frank, this is my mum and dad; Sonia and Dave to you. Dad is just like you used to be Frank, he doesn't say much.

Ella   We should put him on the 'squeeze my hand' treatment; soon have him chatting then wouldn't we, Frank?

Alex   He just said 'yes'.

Ella   Your Alex has been a great little help. He told us a lot he did. Things we couldn't say to one another. Didn't you Alex?

Alex   Sure did.

Sonia   He's a lovely boy.

Ella   Look at him, my little cuckoo.

(*Alex blows a cuckoo call.*)

Ella   Alex, a real cuckoo always cuckoos twice, never once.

Alex   You knew all the time didn't you?

(*Ella smiles.*)

Ella   Goodbye little cuckoo.

(*Alex takes his goodbyes from them all and leaves the nest.*)

Talking Points

(*For discussion in small groups, write each 'Talking Point' on a separate piece of card.*)

1. Why is Alex so disgusted by the idea that Ella and Frank are in love and plan to get married?

2. Why does Alex change his mind about Ella and Frank? Why does he become such a good and useful friend?

3. What makes Alex, Andrew and Allison say such cruel things about the old people in the Home?

4. Do you think that Don and Barbara are a good uncle and aunt to Alex? Were there any times when they should have treated him differently?

5. Do you think Frank's daughter Marjory has good reasons for not wanting her father to marry Ella?

6. At the end of the play, Ella only smiles when Alex asks her if she knew there wasn't a real cuckoo in the tree.

Did she know?

Investigations

1. When Alex gets back to school after the holidays, his English teacher sets the class an essay. The title is:

'What I did this summer'

What does Alex write? Does he tell the full story of the trick he played on Ella and Frank? Is he too ashamed to tell the whole truth about his cruel joke? How does he explain his growing friendship with the old people?

Write Alex's essay for him.

2. Alex and Andrew say some very unkind things about the residents of 'The Grange' old people's home.

'Nobody wants them,' says Alex.
'They're all mental,' says Andrew.

What statements could you come up with that would put the opposite point of view, and that would show elderly people in a good light?

Make two lists, side by side like the one below. In one list, write down what the three As (Alex, Andrew and Allison) say about old people. Look back through the script for examples; pp. 85–88 are the best places to start your research.

In the second list, write down some positive and complimentary comments about old people. Perhaps you have elderly relatives or neighbours who could provide you with examples.

Character	negative comment	positive comment
Andrew	They're all mental (p. 88)	Old people have wonderful memories of the past, even if they're forgetful of today's events

3. Frank's daughter Marjory doesn't want her father to marry again. She's afraid that she'll have to look after Ella when Frank dies.

Imagine that she decides to write to a magazine 'agony aunt' explaining her feelings and asking for advice.

Write her letter. It begins . . .

Dear Janet,
    I'm very worried about my father. He's fallen in love . . .

Then follow this up with the reply that appears in the magazine. It will be addressed to . . .

Dear Marjory . . .

4. Ella wants to write a poem for Frank to celebrate their wedding day.

Working by yourself or with a partner, make up Ella's poem. Remember – she's never been afraid of showing her feelings.

You could take this as your starting point . . .

These are the things I wish you, dear,
On this our wedding day . . .

Give your poem a title.

5. Alex learns to respect Ella and Frank. He begins to understand that they really care for each other. And soon, he begins to care for them. At the start of the holiday he thinks that old people are stupid and that they certainly shouldn't fall in love or get married. At the end of the holiday, he's changed his mind completely.

In pairs, act out the argument that takes place between Alex and a schoolmate when Alex gets back to school. The schoolmate makes an unkind comment about an elderly person. Perhaps the argument starts off by being about one particular event . . . like elderly people causing a queue in a shop because they can't find the right money quickly enough. Then it grows into a more general row.

Show the scenes to the rest of the class and ask people to say if Alex managed to put up a good defence of the elderly.

6. Alex knows what Marjory thinks about her father's plan to marry Ella. So, when Frank gets ill and Marjory goes home, Alex decides to phone her. He wants to tell her she's wrong to stand in her father's way.

He only has enough money to make one short, three-minute call, so he knows that he'd better sort out what he's going to say before he picks up the phone.

In pairs, play out the conversation between Alex and Marjory (or Mike, her husband who feels the same way as she does). Take turns at playing each part. When you've had a chance to play Alex, swap over and play Marjory/Mike. Before you begin, work out what you're going to say as Alex. You have to make your points clearly and briefly if you're going to start persuading Marjory or Mike that the old people should be allowed to live their lives as they please.

You should also decide on the tone of voice you're going to use. And how will you introduce yourself? Your teacher will let you know when the three minutes are up, and that it's time to swap parts.

Later, let the others know how you got on. Do you think you managed to get your points across successfully? Does it seem as if Marjory/Mike might begin to change their mind? Were they annoyed by your phone call, and if they were, how did you find ways to keep them listening?

7. Imagine that your class has been asked to take part in a scheme for getting young and old people in the community to work for each other. In groups, work out the kind of schemes that you think might be set up. How could you be of use to elderly people in your area? How could they be of use to you?

   When you've had time to plan your schemes and list the main contributions of the old and young people to it, present them to the other groups for their comments.

   You may eventually be able to turn this exercise into reality, and set up some of the schemes you suggest.

8. Make a drawing of the three As' tree house. Then work out a detailed plan of the building showing rough measurements, the type and amount of building materials required, and what other tools or equipment you will need to build it.

9. We are never told what 'The Grange' old people's home looks like. We know that it has a big garden, but we don't know anything about the building itself. Working in pairs or in small groups, make a plan of the ground floor of the home.

   Think about the kind of rooms you might find there, e.g. a dining-room, a lounge, an entrance hall, the office, the kitchen, the laundry, toilets, a lift, bedrooms . . . and so on.

   Design your plan to make life easy and comfortable for a group of people living together, and think of ways to let the residents be as independent as possible.

   Label each part of your plan, and maybe add a small drawing of what the house looks like from outside. Later, present your plan to the rest of the class and be prepared to answer any questions or criticisms they may have.

ALL SOULS' EVE

Nona Shepphard

THE CHARACTERS

The family:

Joe
Tom, his brother
Hannah, his mother
Jack, his father
Ginny, his wife

The visitors:

Elizabeth Mottershead
Moll, a farmer's daughter
Maggoty Johnson (male)
Robert Nixon
The Wizard of Alderley Edge (male)
The Gateley Shouter (male)
The Winnington Lady
Elizabeth Southerns, known as **Demdike**

About this play

The play is set in a tiny village in Cheshire, sometime in the eighteenth century.

It takes place at Hallowe'en, a time of trickery and disguise. . .

(A small cottage in rural England; it is dusk.
Hannah enters carrying a taper with which she lights a large, free-standing candle.
She goes and sits in a rocking chair and begins to chant):

Hannah   A soul a soul a soul cake,
     Please good missus, a soul cake,
     An apple, a pear, a plum or a cherry,
     Any old thing to make us all merry,
     One for Peter, two for Paul,
     Three for Him who made us all.

(Jack, her husband, and Tom, her son, enter, carrying wooden planks
with which they set up a table. Ginny, the wife of Hannah's younger son
Joe, enters carrying stools. All three sing the song with Hannah. Then
the two women lay a cloth and bring food, while the two men fetch drink
and candles – all of which are laid on the table.
     As they do so . . .)

Jack   Hannah, I don't know why on earth you're going to all this
     fuss!

Hannah   I know what I'm doing!

Jack   Tom – *you* speak to your mother!

Tom   She never minds what I say.

Jack Go on!

Tom Nobody's going to come, mother . . . you're wasting your time.

Hannah I *know* what I'm doing.

Tom You see? What's the point me talking to her? The only one she'll ever listen to is Joe. But he's gone, mother . . . can you hear me? He's gone!

Hannah He'll come back.

(They stand looking at the finished table.)

Tom All laid out for a party . . . and not a guest in sight.

Ginny Oh shut up, Tom. It's making her feel better. Take no notice, Hannah.

Hannah I'm not.

Tom No, you never do – not where your precious little son Joe's concerned. He won't come.

Hannah And what would you know about what he'll do? You've never understood him . . . you've never liked him even. Your own brother.

Jack Come along, Hannah – let's go . . .

Hannah You just wait and see.

Tom Do you think your husband will come back tonight, Ginny? Will the prodigal son return to grace his mother's party?

Ginny I think you should show some respect.

Jack Apologise to your mother, Tom.

Tom I'm sorry, mother.

Hannah Oh, it's all right, Tom . . . now, you all get along . . . I'll come soon.

*(**Hannah** makes sure that the other three are gone before she goes to a large chest, which is standing in the corner. Out of it she takes a dish of pancakes. She places it on the table.)*

Hannah See what I've made you, pet? Your favourite pancakes
. . . you never could resist your mother's pancakes. Come
home, Joe!

(She goes out. There is silence.
*After some time, **Joe** enters. He stares at the room, and at the table*
as if in a daze. He looks confused as if he were trying to remember
*something. He sees the last dish that **Hannah** has brought out.)*

Joe Pancakes! That's just what I need. And cider too!

(He eats all the dish of pancakes ravenously. He drinks a whole jug of
cider.
He is exhausted. He sits in the rocking chair and closes his eyes.
*A woman enters dressed as **Elizabeth Mottershead**, a sixteenth-*
*century innkeeper. She sees **Joe** and beckons off, whispering . . .)*

Elizabeth Cooee! You can come in now – he's here!

*(A woman and a man enter. The woman, dressed as **Moll** a farmer's*
daughter, is all in white with flowers in her hair. The man, dressed as
***Maggoty Johnson** wears a jester outfit in yellows and reds, carrying*
*bells and a pig's bladder on a stick. All three creep up to **Joe** and*
surround the chair . . . then, altogether, they shout . . .)

Elizabeth
Maggoty   } *(together)* Surprise! Surprise!
Moll

Joe AAAGGHHH!!

Maggoty Welcome! Welcome!

Joe What? You scared the life out of me!

Moll We're so glad to see you.

Joe You are?

Elizabeth Of course we are . . . we didn't know where you were,
we've been so worried about you!

Joe What do you mean?

Maggoty We've all been looking for you for ages.

Joe Why? I don't know you.

Moll   Here, have a drink of cider.

Elizabeth   Don't give him cider . . . he needs a nice cup of camomile tea, after what he's been through.

Joe   I don't get you . . . what am I supposed to have been through?

Elizabeth   You mean you don't know?

Joe   I don't know what you're talking about.

(All three look at each other.)

Maggoty   He doesn't know *us*.

Joe   No, I don't know you . . . I'm right sorry if I should, but I don't . . .

Moll   Please – try and remember – !

Elizabeth   Now, don't be troubling him yet; the important thing is, that he's here with us . . . he's safe now.

Moll   It is wonderful to see you.

Maggoty   Wonderful – it's the answer to my prayers! My good fellow, these two delightful madonnas made me promise that I wouldn't drink a drop until you arrived, and I'm parched . . .

(He starts drinking cider.)

Joe   I think I'm going mad.

Maggoty   Mad? Why mad?

Joe   I think I'm seeing things . . . I've been wandering around I don't know where, for hours or days – I don't know how long and I don't know why . . . and then some crazy people – I don't know who but they're dressed up like players at the Wakes – keep coming at me and shouting 'Surprise, surprise' and keep jabbering on about how worried they've been and how pleased they are to see me . . . and you ask me why I think I'm going mad? You're mad . . . you're crazy – the lot of you!!!

Elizabeth   Now, calm yourself, Joe! Maggoty, don't you dare upset him . . . the Wizard'll have your hide!

Joe   The Wizard? Oh no . . . don't tell me there's more lunatics . . . what's going on?

Elizabeth   Don't you see? He doesn't know what's happened!

Moll   Oh, the poor soul!

Joe   What?

Moll   Sssh! Just you come and sit down.

Elizabeth   And we'll help you remember everything. *Won't we,* Maggoty!

Maggoty   Ah, but of course! Now . . . first things first . . . what night is it?

Joe   I don't know.

Maggoty   Well then – here's a clue – a turnip lantern!

Elizabeth   Another clue – cider and apples!

Moll   And another – candles and cakes!

Maggoty   A night of superstition and magic . . .

Moll   When the other world stalks abroad!

Elizabeth   Look behind you!

(*Joe does, and jumps in fright . . . for crouched on the floor behind him is a man dressed all in black with a white, scowling face. He is dressed as* **Robert Nixon.***)*

Robert   Did you ever see the Devil
With his wooden spade and shovel,
Digging taties by the bushel
With his tail cocked up?

Elizabeth   Don't frighten him, you imbecile!

Joe   I wasn't frightened . . . I knew it was a joke. We used to play tricks like that when I was a lad – going round the lanes in the dark, jumping out at people . . . I used to tie a turnip lantern to a long stick, and bob it up and down at old folk's windows . . . and then we'd come home . . .

Elizabeth   Go on . . .

Joe   And get ourselves up in fancy dress . . .

Moll   Go on . . .

Joe   And come down and tell stories and play games . . .

Maggoty   Go on . . .

Joe   On All Hallows' Eve . . . it's a party! A Hallowe'en party!

Maggoty   Well done, dear boy! I only hope you drink as slowly as
you think . . . I shall be tipsy by morning – cheers!

Moll   And you're the guest of honour.

Joe   I wish I'd known I was going to a party, I'd have guised myself
as well.

Moll   That doesn't matter.

Joe   Let me guess who you've all come as . . .

Maggoty   Very well . . . me first! Tell me if these words ring any
bells –
'Say thou whom chance directs or ease persuades,
To seek the quiet of these sylvan shades,
Here undisturbed and hid from vulgar eyes,
A Wit, Musician, Poet Player lies.'

Joe   I know those words! They're written on a grave! It's the
writing from off a gravestone! We used to play on it in the
woods when I was a boy – 'Under this stone, lie the remains of
Mr. Samuel Johnson, afterwards ennobled with the grand title
of Lord Flame.'

Robert   Otherwise known as Maggoty Johnson.

Joe   Of course . . . the woods are called Maggoty's Woods.

Moll   Wherein, they say, his ghost still walks.

Robert   And if, they say, you wait in those woods in the dead of
night, when the moon is full, you might hear the tinkling of
bells; and if, they say, you follow the sound, you might see a
dark shape of a man, limping ahead of you through the
undergrowth;

(**Maggoty** *jingles his bells.*)

Robert   And if you follow him, you will go deeper and deeper into
the woods, and the footsteps ahead of you will start to run and

so you will start to run and suddenly you will come out into a clearing, and the moon will be shining onto a grave, and there will be no sign of the limping figure, and no sound except the sound of the gravestone, thumping back into place.

(**Maggoty**, *who has been sitting on a wooden chest, gets up. The lid of the chest falls back with a thump.* **Joe** *jumps in fright.*)

Moll Don't frighten him!

Elizabeth We're not here to frighten him, we're here to . . .

Joe What?

Maggoty Have a party! And now you've guessed my disguise – I've come as Maggoty Johnson.

Moll Who joked, sang, fiddled, danced.

Elizabeth And walked on the highest stilts in the North of England!

Robert And fell off them, broke his leg and died.

Maggoty Which explains the limp.

Joe You don't die of a broken leg.

Maggoty No, but you do die of a fever . . .

Joe I had a fever once.

Maggoty Which I caught while I was lying there . . .

Joe I was lying in the dark and my mother . . .

Maggoty Waiting for the wretched leg to heal!

Moll Ssshhh! He's remembering! Go on, Joe . . .

Joe My mother came with some rue tea . . . and after, I was in the dark again, all stuffy and hot, no air . . . can't breathe . . . and then this weird rasping noise, louder and louder, howling and suddenly two huge yellow eyes, cold wet and slimy – all wriggling – and a big mouth opening and coming at me . . . go away! Go away!

Elizabeth Sshh! It's all right . . . sshh! Silly. You had whooping cough that's all. Doesn't everybody know that the best cure for whooping cough is to hold a live frog close to the child's lips to suck the cough away.

Robert The best cure for whooping cough is roast hedgehog!

Maggoty Fried mice!

Moll But neither of these you may look on as nice!

Elizabeth Cure for sore hands – a nice poultice of hot cow manure.

Robert Cure for sore teeth, live woodlice tied round your neck. Cure for dropsy, powdered live cockroaches.

Elizabeth Oh stop!

Robert Cure for ague, a fine fat spider all alive and kicking and eaten with butter.

Elizabeth I'll kick you if you keep on like this . . .

Robert They're proper cures too. How come you're allowed to rabbit on and I'm not? I ate a spider once, with butter, I caught it by its legs . . . it didn't want to go in my mouth but I made it! It was all soft and oily and I could feel its legs wriggling around trying to get out.

Elizabeth It didn't do you much good though, did it? You still starved to death!

Robert At least all the things I said came true – I didn't just go around jabber jabber jabber jaw jaw jawing like a loose-tongued hyena!

Elizabeth You be quiet!

Moll Now stop it!

Robert No wonder you got the Brank!

Maggoty That was cruel . . . even for you.

Elizabeth Why you horrible little . . . !

(She goes to hit him.)

Moll Stop it!

*(**Maggoty** holds her back.)*

Robert   Blabbermouth!

Elizabeth   Dung beetle!

Joe   What's going on?

Moll   *Shut up!!* Both of you.

(They do.)

Joe   What's happening? What are they fighting about?

Moll   They're not really fighting – they're just pretending. Aren't you? *Well*, aren't you?

(They look sullen but shamefaced.)

Robert }
Elizabeth } Yes.

Joe   They didn't look like they were pretending.

Maggoty   Of course they were . . . er . . . it's a party . . . and they were both giving you clues.

Joe   What do you mean – clues?

Moll   Clues as to who they've come to the party as.

Joe   Well, I'm none the wiser.

Maggoty   Think, dear boy, think.

*(He indicates **Robert**.)*

Maggoty   A man with a white face, staring eyes, surly manner, rude speech, whose words come true and who starved to death?

Moll   Can you guess?

Joe   No.

Robert   Simpleton!

Joe   What did you say?

Moll   Robert Nixon! He's come as Robert Nixon.

Joe   And who's he when he's at home?

Maggoty   The Nostradamus of Neston! Cheshire's own prophet.

Joe   Oh you call yourself a prophet, do you? And have any of your prophesies come true?

Robert   The crows will drink the blood of many nobles and the North will rise against the South.

Moll   That was the Wars of the Roses.

Robert   Between a rick and two trees, a famous battle shall be.

Moll   The Battle of St Albans between Elstree, Edwinstree and Rickmansworth.

Maggoty   He got so famous, he was taken up to the King's court because of his supernatural gifts, and he knew. He knew what was going to happen to him.

Robert   He's coming . . . he's on the road for me! I shall be clem'd!

Moll   And he was right . . . death was coming for him. The servants at the court called him 'Cretin! Lack-brain! Half-wit! Drivelling idiot!' and they locked him in a closet and forgot about him. He died three days later.

Joe   Nasty!

Robert   Yes, nasty! Very, very nasty!

Elizabeth   It was good riddance, I say.

Robert   And it was good riddance to you when *you* died! You got the Brank! You got the Brank!

Elizabeth   Why you . . .

Maggoty   Steady, Elizabeth! Remember why we're here!

Elizabeth   Of course . . .

Joe   I really don't know who you're meant to be.

Elizabeth   Elizabeth Mottershead, landlady of the Blue Posts Inn in Stockport.

Moll   Renowned throughout England for her courage in uncovering a plot that saved thousands of Irish lives!

Robert   But she couldn't save her own! She got the Brank 'cos she talked too much!

Elizabeth   One more word out of you and I'll . . .

Joe   So what is this Brank?

Moll   Sssssh. Let's not talk about it.

Joe   Is it like a spank? You got a good hiding, did you?

Maggoty   Don't make stupid remarks about things you know nothing about.

Joe   Don't talk to me like that! It's my party, *remember?*

Elizabeth   Oh tell him – it can't hurt me now.

Maggoty   The Brank, dear boy, was a fiendishly clever invention for the control of a shrewish woman; it was a kind of iron helmet, which went over the culprit's head, having a tongue plate which acted as a gag and a chain behind, by which she could be led through the streets like an animal.

Moll   The Stockport Brank may especially interest you, for the gag was swollen so as to fill the mouth, and had three sharp pins on top with two more pointing backwards, and two below, so that every time the tongue was moved, the utmost agony was caused; the chain was at the front which ensured that the mouth was torn to ribbons every time the man leading it gave a tug.

Maggoty   Heard enough?

Joe   Yes.

Maggoty   Satisfied now?

Joe   I'm sorry, I didn't mean –

Elizabeth   When he brought it home, I thought it was for the dog, which would have been bad enough, and then he put it on me!

(There is a pause. They are all quiet and sad.)

Joe   Look, what's going on here?

Moll   You wanted to know . . . so we told you. And now you've upset her.

Joe   I've upset her? They were clues – that's what you said – guess who they are – that's what you said – it's a party you said –

they're pretending – well she doesn't look like she's pretending
. . . and I've had enough of all this . . . I'm tired and I don't
know what's happening, so you can all clear out. Party's over!

*(Suddenly, the lid of the chest in the corner starts to rise . . . and a voice
– of the **Wizard** – is heard coming from inside.)*

Voice   Oh no. The party isn't over yet, Joe. It isn't nearly over.

*(As they watch, a man sits up in the chest, and stands. He is very tall,
with long white flowing hair. He is dressed as a **Wizard**.)*

Joe   I can't stand any more of this!

Wizard   I'm afraid you have no choice, Joe. You have to stay here
with us.

Joe   Why do I? Why?

Wizard   You have to stay and remember what brought you here.

Joe   But I don't remember anything.

Wizard   Oh yes you do . . . you have already remembered quite a
lot . . . you've eaten your mother's pancakes, you've
remembered Hallowe'en pranks and playing as a boy in
Maggoty's woods and having a fever and being cured . . .

Joe   But nothing else!

Wizard   Which is why I have come. To jog your memory still
further.

Joe   Yes . . . yes . . . I have seen you before!

*(The other four all look at **Joe** eagerly. All speak together.)*

All   Where?

Wizard   Be quiet, all of you! All you four seem to have achieved is
to upset and confuse the poor boy. Leave it to me! Now, Joe,
think! You found a picture once rolled up on the ground . . .
you were only a boy . . .

Joe   Yes . . . I liked the colours in it . . . they were bright and
new and I kept it under my pillow . . . the man in the picture
looked just like you!

Wizard   And what happened to this treasured picture?

Joe   One day it wasn't there any more. I cried.

Wizard   Who had taken it, Joe?

Joe   I can't remember . . . oh yes I can . . . my brother . . . it was my brother . . . Tom! He took it!

Wizard   Why had he taken it?

Joe   Because . . . because he always wanted anything that was mine. Always.

Wizard   And what did he do with the picture?

Joe   He threw it in the fire . . . and so we had a big, big fight – I got a black eye . . . but he had a broken nose!

Wizard   And did you often fight with your brother Tom?

Joe   We were always fighting over something. My mother tried to comfort me about the picture being burnt up, by telling me the story of Wizard of Alderley Edge . . . he was the one in the picture, see? He was a mighty wizard and tutor to King Arthur and he's the Guardian of the Iron Gates, which lead down into caverns in the rock, miles under Alderley Edge . . .

Wizard   And in them lies the sleeping army of King Arthur – waiting for the Wizard's call to rise up again, and defend the land.

Joe   Fancy you coming dressed like my old picture!

Wizard   You see, I have helped you remember something.

Joe   Oh yes . . . and there's more . . . I remember sitting around the fire at Hallowe'en in the dark eating roasted chestnuts and pancakes, and my mother and father would tell me and Tom ghost stories to frighten us! And one year my mother told us a funny story about this ghost –

Wizard   Who used to pop out of his grave in a northern churchyard and cry –

(A voice moans from off.)

Shouter   Oh dear, oh dear, wa-a-a-tered milk! Wa-a-a-tered milk!

Joe   That's it . . . how did you know?

Wizard   Oh, I know most ghost stories from around here.

(*A little man rushes on, dressed in a long white nightshirt and hat carrying a pail of milk and a pail of water.*)

Joe   They used to call him the Gately Shouter!

Shouter   Milk and water sold I ever,
    Weight and measure gave I never!

(*Joe laughs.*)

Joe   This is more like a party! I like your costume.

(*The others look relieved.*)

Elizabeth   He's a very vulgar bogey.

Joe   He was a tradesman, see, who used to water down his milk 'cos he was so fond of money. And when he died –

Shouter   Old Scrat, the Devil, got me! And he burnt me so I used to run around the lanes . . . squeaking and jibbering and frightening folks to death! He he he! But then they got a parson onto me, and all the folks got round him, and they drew towards one another in a ring like, and kept coming closer, till at last they got me in a corner in the churchyard by the yew tree, and the parson was on the grave and he whips out a bit of chalk, and draws a holy ring round me, and all the folks join hands and pray, desperate like, and the parson hops about and bangs the Book till he's all of a muck sweat! And I got littler and littler till I fair sweated away, like a snail when it's been salted, and they drove the Devil out of me, and now I'm quiet as a mouse. And I live under the big stone near the parson's gate. HE! HE! HE!

(*He scuttles off, chuckling.*)

Joe   I like that story.

(*As the **Shouter** goes off, a woman comes on. She is dressed as a lady going to a ball, and carries a lancet – a doctor's sharp instrument for making surgical cuts – and a large wooden box. She places the box on the table and opens it up. There is a mirror in the lid. It is a musical box and when she opens it up, we hear strains of ball music. She looks at herself in the mirror.*)

Lady Did you like my story too?

Joe Who are you?

Lady I am the Winnington Lady.

Wizard The pale ghost of the niece of Lord Penrhyn, who haunts Winnington Hall, still looking for her lover . . .

Lady My uncle is giving a grand ball for the county . . . I must look my best, for my lover is to be here tonight – my skin must be white as milk and soft as a snowflake – but no! It is flushed, flushed pink with excitement! What shall I do?

Wizard She took a lancet, determined to bleed herself a little; not too much . . . she didn't want to faint . . .

Lady But I must hurry, I can hear the waltzes already beginning . . .

Wizard Her hand trembled as the blade flashed in the candlelight, seeking her vein . . .

Moll Not too fast . . . not too fast . . .

Lady But the music, I can hear it . . . he'll be looking for me to dance! We shall dance until dawn!

Moll Her hand slipped!

Lady Ah! So much blood! Help me! Somebody help me!

Wizard She ran out onto the balcony . . . and there under the gaze of the helpless guests – she bled to death.

*(The **Lady** has pretended to die. All the others sigh.)*

Joe Ugh! That's a horrible story. My mother never told me that story . . .

Lady No, not your mother . . . someone else told you . . . another woman. A young woman.

Joe A young woman told me that story about you?

Lady *Yes.* Don't you remember?

Joe I was . . . *we* were walking down a moonlit road. Past an old hall . . .

Lady   Winnington Hall . . .

Joe   That's right! We'd just crossed over the Farndon Bridge . . . and we'd heard cries . . .

Wizard   And she said they were the cries of the ghosts of two little boys who were drowned there . . .

Joe   Yes, she did . . . this young woman I was walking with . . . who is she?

Lady   What did you reply to her, Joe. Remember exactly what you said!

Joe   I said, 'Don't be stupid, Ginny, there're no such things as ghosts!'

Lady   Ginny.

Joe   How could I have forgotten her? My own wife. How could I?

Elizabeth   Don't worry, pet . . . you've had a shock, that's all.

Joe   Ginny . . . I'd just met her that very day at the Summer Wake at Knutsford . . . yes . . . I'd been chosen to play Adam in the procession, and she'd been chosen to play Eve . . . we felt foolish at first . . . but then we got talking . . .

Lady   And you liked each other . . . very much.

Joe   And we spent the whole of the day together, and then I walked her home, which was when she told me your story.

Wizard   And when did you see her again, Joe?

Joe   I can't remember . . . I can't remember . . .

Maggoty   Well, never mind, dear boy. That's what we're here for. Ladies! Let us play that time honoured Cheshire game of 'lifting'. Get into pairs!

Wizard   I'd better summon up a partner! A witch for a wizard! Elizabeth! Elizabeth!

(*A very old woman comes on. She is very frail and dressed in rags as* **Demdike**. *She can hardly see.*)

Wizard   This is Elizabeth Southerns, known as Demdike.

Demdike What do you want?

Wizard We're playing games . . . I need a partner.

Demdike I'm too old for games – get away with you.

Joe You're no witch!

Wizard Now, now, Elizabeth, you know why I've called you here . . . we are playing the game of 'lifting' to refresh our young friend's memory . . . help us!

Demdike I am a witch! I am! Devil came to me like a boy with a coat . . . half black, half brown! He came to me as a black cat or a brown dog to suck blood from under my arm . . . the man saw the spot – he jabbed at me with a spike! *He* knew I was a witch . . . he put me in prison for it!

Joe Well, I don't believe it.

Moll Stop teasing her.

Joe I'm not – she looks nothing like a witch.

Maggoty Oh and what are witches supposed to look like? Warty old hags with black cloaks and pointy hats on broomsticks, flying round Pendle Hill with black cats and cauldrons?

Joe No . . . but they're supposed to be powerful and frightening, so the stories say when you're a kid! She doesn't look like she could harm a fly!

Wizard She couldn't. Her crime was being an old, poor, near sightless beggarwoman, who used herbal remedies, spells and charms . . . an easy target for the witchfinders, don't you think?

Joe Don't tell me *she* was put in prison?

Robert Oh yes . . . her and ten others! No heat! No light shining in! Shut up! Just like me in my cupboard . . .

Wizard April 1612. Elizabeth Southerns, otherwise known as Demdike, died in Lancaster jail, where she was awaiting death for being a witch.

Demdike All the others got hanged!

Elizabeth   The others included her daughter, grandson and granddaughter, hanged a mile from the castle.

Joe   You poor old soul.

Demdike   Never mind me. It's you! *You* poor old soul!

Joe   Me? I'm all right . . . I just don't know anything, that's all.

Maggoty   Which is precisely why we were playing 'lifting'. In Cheshire, every Easter, the men lift the women on a Monday . . . it's Monday!

*(All the men except **Joe** lift a woman.)*

Maggoty   And the women lift the men on a Tuesday . . . it's Tuesday!

(All the women lift their partners.)

Maggoty   Strangers to our customs have often complained about being surrounded by gangs of women and hoisted from the ground . . . although many men have been known to enjoy it very much!

(They all laugh.)

Joe   Oh I know why you're doing this! It was the next time I saw Ginny . . . of course. Tom and I took the decorated chair round to her house in Farndon. She'd left the window open specially. We lifted her up in the chair, and she gave me a kiss!

Wizard   And then what happened?

Joe   I had a fight with Tom because he kissed her as well. He said she was the most beautiful girl he had ever seen.

Moll   But it was you she liked.

Joe   Yes. The following May, a gang of us went out May birching into the woods, and me and Ginny just sort of got lost.

Elizabeth   Very likely.

Moll   And you asked her to marry you.

Joe   And she said yes.

Wizard   And then what happened, Joe?

Joe   We were married of course.

Moll   And was she happy?

Joe   Of course she was.

Moll   And were you faithful?

Joe   Yes.

Moll   You're lying!

Joe   I'm not. I was . . . I am faithful. Who have you been talking to?

Moll   I haven't been talking to anyone. I speak because I know about betrayal . . . I have felt like your Ginny must have felt. That is why I have been brought here to be with you.

Joe   What happened to you?

Elizabeth   Her name is Moll – a farmer's daughter, who fell in love with Will, the lad who ran the ferry over the river at Runcorn.

Moll   He asked me to marry him, and I said yes.

Elizabeth   But Will was light of love –

Moll   He turned from me to somebody else.

Robert   Nasty! Very nasty!

Moll   Sssh, dear, I'm all right now.

Elizabeth   So, one sorrowful November night, she wandered to the riverside, a wild despair in her eyes, and uttering a low, plaintive cry, muttered feebly,

Moll   'The waves will be kinder to me than the world.'

Elizabeth   She disappeared without a struggle or a cry.

Maggoty   The next morning, Will was struck dumb with terror and remorse when, rowing across the river, he saw a tress of drowned black hair. His conscience accused him of being the murderer of the fair girl!

Robert   He was too!

Elizabeth   He could not rest. For days he neither slept nor ate . . .

Robert   Serves him right!

Maggoty   And then, one morning, his body was found washed up at the castle rock.

Robert   Good riddance!

Moll   All the village mourned, and his *new* sweetheart decorated his hearse!

(Everybody is quiet, looking at Joe.)

Joe   Why are you all looking at me like that? I'm very sorry that you had such a bad time and all that, but that wasn't the way it was with me and Ginny. *I* didn't have another sweetheart like this Will character. I swear I didn't!

(They still look at him. He starts to remember vividly.)

Joe   *She* didn't believe me either . . . Ginny didn't . . . somebody must have been spreading lies about me – to her . . . she'd never have thought it on her own. And then, one night, in the small hours, I hear a trumpet blown to call the Stang together – and I hear it coming closer – kettles and pots beating, whistles, horns and trumpets blowing, getting louder and louder, and then I knew . . . It wasn't some other's house they were going to stand outside and read rhymes about adultery and keep them awake . . . No. They were coming for me! And it wasn't true! Who'd been spreading lies? They came three times, and by the third night, I couldn't bear to hear Ginny crying any more, so I went out. They had two straw figures which they held up and set fire to, and then this man starts the rhyme – and I knew then it was him – he was the one who'd been telling those stories – he had his back to me, so I wrenched him round – he had this straw mask on, hiding his face, so I got hold of the corner of it and I ripped it off and he raised this spade above his head and brought it down, and I could feel the blood pouring into my brain – that's when I lost track – I can't remember anything else.

Wizard   Are you sure? Nothing else?

Maggoty   Nothing else?

Moll   Nothing else . . . before that? About the house?

Demdike   A sparrow tapping on the window? A sudden crack in the furniture? Bells ringing suddenly? Clocks stopping? Owls screeching?

Joe   Yes, yes, I do! But that's death – omens of death – oh dear God, not Ginny! Is that what you were trying to tell me, with Moll's story? Ginny's dead, isn't she?

Elizabeth   Now don't upset yourself. We're here to help you.

Joe   Tell me, please!

Moll   Ssh. Come and lie down here – she's not dead – quiet now.

Elizabeth   Lie down . . . still and quiet.

(They lie him down on the long table which they have cleared. They stand around him.)

Wizard   Tell us. Is there anything else you remember?

Joe   A blinding light, so bright I can't see . . . and then the outside of a house . . . a man sits on a stool . . . it is the Sineater!

Demdike   The Sineater has come from the woods, nobody in the village can look at him . . . he sits on his stool . . . takes money, eats bread, drinks wine . . . The Sineater says,

Robert   'I eat the sins of the dead. I eat adultery and deceit.'

Joe   Yes, yes, and then inside the house – too far away to see clearly . . . a white space, people moving around it . . . putting things on it . . . money at the top, something at a dish in the middle . . . then one by one . . . going up to it and touching it – I'm closer now . . . first my father, then my mother, Where's Ginny? Where is she? Oh *there* she is! She's *not* dead . . . thank God!

Wizard   No, *she's* not dead.

Joe   Then who is?

Wizard   Keep remembering and you will know.

Joe   Ginny's crying! She's very distressed! Someone's putting their arms around her . . . but . . . it's not me! It's Tom. My brother, Tom.

*(The others have spread the white tablecloth over **Joe** as a shroud. They place money at his head and a dish of salt on his stomach.)*

Joe I remember now . . . it was my brother, Tom, who was the man with the straw mask on, who lifted the spade! It was my brother, Tom, who hit me!

(He jumps up from the table, sending everything flying. He realises what they have been making him remember.)

Joe Dead? Me? Me? Is that what you're telling me? Me – dead? Ha! That's the best joke of the night! We've been dressing up . . . *pretending* to be ghosts . . .

Wizard We're not pretending, Joe.

Moll I *am* Moll.

Elizabeth I *am* Elizabeth Mottershead.

Maggoty I *am* Maggoty Johnson.

Robert I *am* Robert Nixon.

Wizard This is All Souls' Eve. All Souls' Eve is the night –

Demdike When the living leave out food for us –

All The *dead!*

Joe But I'm not one of you – I'm not dead.

Elizabeth Listen, Joe . . . when somebody dies a sudden, violent death, they are in shock and pain . . . so much shock that they often don't realise they've died . . . they need help to come to terms with it.

Wizard And I chose these seven souls to come and help you, because they all died deaths like that . . . they've told you . . . you heard their stories.

Joe I can't be dead.

Maggoty Well, this is your house, isn't it?

Joe Yes.

Maggoty Where are your family?

Joe I don't know . . . I . . . they must be in bed. Yes that's it!

(He shouts.)

Joe   Mother! Ginny! Wake up!

(There is silence.)

Wizard   They are in church, Joe. They are praying all night long for the soul of their recently departed −

Elizabeth   Son.

Moll   Husband.

Robert   Brother.

*(At last **Joe** realises it is the truth. He speaks to **Demdike**.)*

Joe   So, I *am* a poor old soul after all! I never knew.

Demdike   Not so bad, is it?

Maggoty   And look on the bright side, dear boy . . . you'll have us for company forever more!

Joe   But my family . . . Ginny . . . I must stay and see them.

Elizabeth   Oh no, not this again. Why do they always say this?

Maggoty   They never learn, do they?

Elizabeth   You'll only get upset − they can't see you or hear you.

Joe   Please!

Wizard   You may stay just this once. But not for long! Come away, all other souls! The sun is nearly up.

*(They all go out, leaving **Joe** alone. The sun starts to shine in. **Tom** enters, as if he has been running. He sees the mess.)*

Tom   Well, well, well . . . you came back with a vengeance, didn't you, little brother?

Joe   Yes, I did.

Tom   I wonder if you really were here last night.

*(**Joe** blows out the large candle. **Tom** sees it go out.)*

Tom   Ah. So you are here . . . well here or not, you can't bother me any more.

(*Ginny enters.*)

Ginny   Who are you talking to, Tom.

Joe   Me, Ginny. He's talking to me!

Tom   I was just saying a prayer for the dead.

(*Ginny sees the mess. She gasps.*)

Ginny   Look at this! They've been . . . I wonder if Joe was here . . .

Joe   I *am* here, Ginny. Can't you hear me?

Ginny   I've never seen such a mess on this night before.

Tom   Well, at least little brother's not here to make a mess of your life any more.

Joe   No, you saw to that, didn't you, Tom?

Ginny   Tom! Don't talk that way of the dead. You sound as if you hated him.

Tom   I'm sorry – it's just the way he treated you.

Ginny   It was just the way he was.

Joe   I'm sorry if I hurt you, Ginny.

(*Jack and Hannah enter.*)

Hannah   He's been here, I know it! Joe's been here.

Jack   Now don't you go imagining things, Hannah!

Hannah   He's been here, I tell you.

Ginny   How can you be so sure?

Hannah   He's eaten all his favourite pancakes.

Tom   That doesn't prove anything.

Hannah   Don't argue with me, Thomas. I *know*.

Joe   Yes. She does.

Jack   Well, Hannah, his soul must be at rest now . . . we've prayed all night, he's eaten food at his old home and his murderer has been punished.

Joe What? He's standing right there!

Hannah What? That old tramp?

Jack Yes . . . the one Tom caught. The men strung him up last night.

Ginny So quickly? But nothing had been proved.

Hannah He didn't look as if he could harm a fly. He was so old and frail. Are they sure he did it?

Tom He was guilty all right . . . he was so drunk he didn't remember what he was doing. He admitted as much to me.

Jack So justice has been done.

Joe The poor old soul! I expect *he'll* be needing our help now! Justice has not been done.

(He gets up from the rocking chair. All the living see is a chair moving on its own. All gasp or scream.)

Hannah There look! I told you. He's with us!

Tom Ginny, come out of here.

Ginny Tom, you look dreadful.

Jack I think this calls for a drink.

Tom Don't worry, Ginny, I'm looking after you now.

Joe I'm sure you are.

*(**Ginny** pauses, listens for a moment then looks at **Tom** with a strange expression on her face. All leave except **Hannah** and **Joe**.)*

Hannah I know you're here, Joe. And I can feel that you're not troubled any more. Go in peace.

*(**Maggoty** pops his head round the door.)*

Maggoty Have you seen enough? We're all waiting for you.

Joe I'm coming.

(He takes a last look at his mother and his home.)

Joe Yes. I'm all right now.

Talking Points

(For discussion in small groups, write each 'Talking Point' on a separate piece of card.)

1. Who murdered Joe? How did he die?

2. Who was blamed for Joe's death? On whose evidence? Was this person given a fair trial?

3. Why was Joe murdered?

4. Why did the Stang come to Joe's house? What was he accused of?

5. Why doesn't Joe know that he is dead?

6. Why are these particular ghosts chosen to visit him? What have they got in common with Joe?

7. Why does Joe say that he's all right at the end of the play? Why does he go away?

8. Will Tom go free?

   Will Ginny marry Tom?

9. What would you like to happen next?

Investigations

1. Choose one of the ghosts in the play and write their story – in their own words.

2. Write the next part of *All Souls' Eve* either as a story or as a playscript. It could tell us what happens in the real world or in the spirit world – or it could be about a meeting between the two worlds.

3. Imagine that you have been asked to help make up a *Dictionary of Ghosts*. You are an expert on the ghosts of Lancashire and Cheshire – the ones you've been reading about in the play. Your job is to write a short piece on each of the ghosts mentioned, including Joe.

   Start your detective work by looking back through the script and the cast list and arrange the ghosts' names in alphabetical order. (Decide if you're going to put surnames first, like this . . .

   JOHNSON, Maggoty
   NIXON, Robert

   and also decide how and where you'll fit in the names of those ghosts with titles – like The Gately Shouter.)

Use the script to find out as much as you can about each of the ghosts. Make your dictionary as fact-filled as possible . . . and maybe include a drawing of each ghost.

4. Twenty years later, the truth about Joe's murder has been discovered. Ginny decides to put a new tombstone on his grave. A verse will be carved on the stone, telling of Joe's innocence and explaining how the truth came to light.

Write the verse for Ginny, but keep it quite short so that it will fit onto the tombstone. You can use modern English or eighteenth-century English similar to the writing on Maggoty's gravestone (p. 110).

If you do a first draft of your verse, you could later transfer it to a cut-out of the tombstone. Make the 'stone' look old by painting white paper with cold tea and giving it ragged edges. When it's dry, write your verse on the 'stone' in suitable lettering.

5. Whether or not you believe in ghosts, there's no doubt that stories about them can be very exciting! They give you great freedom to travel in time and space: nothing seems to stand in the way of ghosts . . . not even walls!

Write a modern ghost story. It could be frightening or funny, and though it starts off in the present day it could take us to days gone by . . . or even to days that are yet to come!

6. Bring Tom to trial!

As a class, become the court that will accuse him of Joe's murder.

Appoint a judge – or judges, members of the jury, lawyers to put the case for and against Tom. Other members of the class can play the witnesses who have evidence to offer in the case. These could be members of Joe's family, or members of the Stang who were at Joe's house on the night of his death. Look through the script for clues to help you prepare the trial. What new evidence might have come to light that will help to convict Tom? What defence will Tom put up?

The members of the jury should give their verdict according to what they hear in the courtroom. It would be best to ask people from another class – who don't know the play – to come and be an unbiased jury.

If Tom is found guilty, what will his punishment be?

7. In small groups, make a waxworks museum about the ghost stories in *All Souls' Eve*. *You* become the figures in the wax exhibits!

Choose which story you want to work on and pick out a good, strong part of the story to make into your waxwork.

Show the exhibits to the rest of the class. Perhaps these exhibits are very advanced models that can come to life and repeat the action of the scene over and over again – with sounds and words.

Make a title for your exhibit.

8. Imagine that your school is putting on a production of *All Souls' Eve*. Design a poster for the play. Remember that it is a murder mystery as well as a ghost story. Which viewpoint will you want to stress in your poster?

9. Design the costumes for all or some of the characters in the play. You'll need to read through the script to look for clues about the way they are dressed. Begin by making a list of the characters you are interested in and list the pages on which their costumes are described. Some research will probably be necessary. Your school library may have books on period costume or paintings of the times featured in the play. Joe and his family are living in the eighteenth century, but the ghosts are from earlier times.

Make a display of your costume designs.

10. The play takes place at Hallowe'en, the feast of All Souls' Eve. There are traditions associated with many festivals, such as Christmas, Easter, Diwali, Passover . . . Some are celebrated all over the world. Some are only local.

In groups, make a chart listing the festivals that you know about, and say how they are celebrated.

Are they all well known, or do you think that some of them just take place in your area?

11. Your own family – or circle of friends – can probably come up with lots of strange and wonderful stories. Most people enjoy telling them . . . if you can catch them at the right time! Search out some people with strange stories to tell. Then tape-record their stories, so you can write them down and collect them in a class book of *Strange Tales*.

SOME BACKGROUND TO THE PLAY

All Souls' Eve is based on characters, stories, rhymes and traditions from Lancashire and Cheshire. On All Souls' Eve, which we now know as Hallowe'en, people would lay out food and drink for the souls of the dead, and spend the night in church praying for them.

Elizabeth Southerns died in prison accused of witchcraft. Robert Nixon was holed up and left to starve. The writing on Maggoty Johnson's gravestone (p. 110) is taken from fact. Some characters, like Moll and the Wizard of Alderley Edge are more based on folk-tale, but the tales themselves are often taken from real-life characters and incidents.

The Brank (p. 112) was used as a weapon of torture for women. The Stang (p. 124) really took place. Groups of village men would visit the houses of people accused of doing wrong. They would stand outside the house making a terrible din and burning straw figures.

The Sineater (p. 125) came and 'ate' the sins of the dead so that they could rest in peace.